An Actor's Business

How Show Business Works
&
How To Market Yourself As An Actor
No Matter Where You Live

An Actor's Business

How Show Business Works
&
How To Market Yourself As An Actor
(No Matter Where You Live)

Andrew Reilly

Venture Press
Fort Lauderdale, FL

This book is for my mother.
Hi, Mom!

Table of Contents

What This Book Will do For You

If you are considering making acting a career, then I wrote this book for you. Read it, and when you are done you will have learned two very important things:

- Whether or not you really want an acting career.
- If you do, how you can build that acting career from the ground up, no matter where you live.

I am an actor myself, as well as a writer, director, and teacher of acting. I began acting in community theatre some time ago, and for years acting was just an enjoyable hobby. When I finally decided to turn professional, I got some formal training, specifically a Master of Fine Arts degree in acting from the University of South Carolina and then further study at the Folger Conservatory. I did regional theatre work, TV commercials, and some day-player roles in feature films which were shooting on location in the Southeast. I saved some money and set out for Los Angeles. After a year there I got a notice from the Screen Actors Guild that I was going to have to pay an increase in my union dues because of my earnings as an actor.

I immediately called the union and told the lady in bookkeeping that there must be some mistake. My total earnings as a film actor for that year, I told her, came to only $6,800. She quickly informed me that this was, comparatively speaking, quite a large sum. It seems that I had made more money in film that year than 85% of the members of the L.A. local of the Screen Actors Guild.

Needless to say, I was stunned—but I should not have been. For some months preceding this bit of news, I had been trading notes with other actors on the difficulties of actually earning one's living as an actor. The consensus? Lacking the kind of marketing skills I will share with you in this book, such a career is virtually impossible.

My conclusion? While professional training programs in this

country are turning out some fine actors, most to them don't have the faintest idea how to get started in the business. As strange as it may seem, the marketing of one's talents is just not a part of the curriculum in most acting schools. This is a crucial omission. No professional training program should call itself that without a real study of the "business of acting," of the proven ways that you can sell your talent, get work as an actor and build a career in your chosen field.

This book tells you about work-getting and self-marketing tips and techniques that most actors have to pick up piecemeal, over a long period of time, if they manage to pick them up at all. It is actually a kind of marketing manual of the sort that would be used to sell insurance or real estate. This book will help you decide what you are selling, how to find and convince people to buy what you are selling, and how to keep track of it all.

An Actor's Business can save you three years of your acting life. An actor is really engaged in a kind of small business, and statistics show that 60 percent of small businesses fail before their third year. This is also just about the length of time it takes for most actors to leave New York or L.A. and return to Charlotte or Des Moines, disillusioned and unaware of why they failed.

Before an actor becomes established and becomes one of the five percent of his peers who earn their entire living by acting, he or she has almost invariably stuck it out for at least five years. When you have finished this book you will be prepared to join that five percent.

- You will know how to turn yourself into a small acting business.
- You will have an understanding of how you fit into the larger stream of commerce that is show business.
- And if you then decide to go for it, you will have at least a fighting chance of becoming that one professional actor in twenty that makes all of his or her money acting.

Yours in the audition line,
Andrew Reilly

I

The State of the Art

More people are afraid of getting up in front of an audience than of anything else, including snakes or heights. So why do actors do it? Actually, yes, we are a bit nuts, like most creative people. There's actually a theory that creativity is nature's compensatory mechanism for coping with madness. Some actors seem to cope with life by dredging up very private parts of themselves for public display. Sometimes you can get paid for that; however, most professional actors prefer to make a living by advancing stories without causing distractions. (We'll come back to this again, many times.)

Laurence Olivier is reported to have said that there is only one reason anyone becomes an actor: "Look at me! Look at me! Look at me!" Actors are usually out-going and seem to require a kind of regular validation of their worth from other people.

Many pretty women give the business a try, "just to see," as they are fond of saying, and find that there are actually not that many roles for very pretty women and tremendous competition for such roles as there are. Cool guys who plan to become the next action hero will encounter the same sort of problem, whereas an actor who can play the romantic lead's friend and confidant has a much better chance of working regularly.

Yes, there are quite a number of gay men who become actors, but the necessary combination of being both sensitive and out-going is probably more characteristic of the artistic community in general than of the gay community. Outgoing "character-types" find in show business a community which accepts them, and which might actually pay them for being fat or bald, assuming, of course, that they can act.

What is the main difference between an amateur and a professional actor? An amateur is defined in the dictionary as one who does something only for the love of it. The word "amateur" does not mean

11

someone who is second rate. America's community theaters are blessed with people who act for the love of it, and some have more talent and more skill than many professional actors. After all, a professional can be defined as simply someone who does something for money, with all that this implies, although an actor can rarely last long in show business if he or she doesn't do it at least as much for love as for money.

It is regretable that many actors who decide to become professionals do so with the idea of becoming stars. They think that this is what "making it" means, and they are sadly wrong.

A star is someone who can get his or her name above the title in a feature film, a TV show, or in lights on a Broadway marquee. This "ability" is not always because of talent, skill, beauty, or charisma, though these things certainly help, but rather because of an unpredictable desire on the part of the public to watch this person. Most people do not go to the movies to see a story so much as to see their favorite stars in a given situation. The rest of the actors involved in the production just do their jobs and advance the story. If they advance enough stories they can make a good living, even though no one but people in the industry and the folks in their home towns may know their names. Actors who work like this regularly have indeed "made it," and often lead happier, fuller lives than stars. They retire with a pension from the Screen Actor's Guild, or one of the other performer's unions, and a thousand memories of small victories, artfully achieved.

No one, including the heads of the seven major studios, can accurately predict who is going to become a star, or why. The decision-makers at United Artists, for example, were sure that Kris Kristopherson was going to become a star, so they put him in a little something called *Heaven's Gate*. The public, however, didn't think Kristopherson was going to be a star, and the movie lost so much money that the studio went belly up. United Artists was later sold by its parent corporation, Transamerica, to MGM, which wanted to acquire UA's distribution network. And Kris Kristopherson? I'm told that Willie Nelson still returns his phone calls.

At any given time there are less than one hundred stars, and more than one hundred thousand union actors. The actual membership breakdown will be covered in a later chapter. There are also an estimated two hundred thousand more actors hoping to get into the unions at any given time, and most of them will have given up within three years, to be replaced by two hundred thousand more. Such people, as well as most union actors, might be called "wannabees." You see them striking poses at parties and cafes, complaining that the entertainment industry doesn't appreciate real talent. If such person is a friend of yours, suggest this book, even though he will probably not get past this chapter. I occasionally give marketing seminars for actors, and have discovered a sad truth: most "wannabees" care more about clinging to their affectations than about doing good work or getting the check.

Actors who go into the business with the idea of becoming stars might as well base their careers on winning the lottery. "But," you say, "an actor needs to believe in himself." That's true, son, but in order to make a living as an actor, he needs to believe the right things about himself. It's not enough to have a dream. He or she also needs a plan.

Want to act professionally? Read on MacDuff, and keep your sense of humor. After all, it ain't nothin' but another job.

An Actor's Real Work
What does a professional actor do? "She acts," you say. Sorry, that response is too vague, and is only a part of the truth. That is like saying "a real estate salesman sells houses."

The sucessful real estate agent spends most of her time canvassing — on the phone, in the newspaper, behind the wheel of a car, or on foot. A very small portion of her time is actually spent showing houses to potential buyers, and an even smaller portion is spent watching contracts being signed. (A real estate agent who watches one such signing a month is doing rather well, and is probably among the ten percent in the field that sell ninety percent of the real estate.)

The parallels between a career in sales and a career in acting will become more apparent as we move along. A successful actor spends about as much time canvassing and as little time showing the product (auditioning) as a real estate salesman, and, as in real estate, about ten percent of the professionals get about ninety percent of the work. This is not because they are necessarily more talented than the rest. It is because each has turned his talent into a marketable skill and has learned how to canvass the market for people willing to buy that skill. Such actors do not wait for a talent agent to get them work, and the reasons why will become clearer in the chapter on talent agents.

Ultimately, whether the actor or the talent agent arranges for

13

an audition, the pro knows that the actor's job is to advance a story in the best possible way without causing distractions—no more, no less—and her ability to do that is what she is selling. This is true whether an actor has one line or a hundred lines of dialogue. It is also true for extras.

Playwrights and screenplay writers do not write stories to showcase actors. It's true that Hollywood development people often ruin stories in order to showcase stars, but we can not help that. Besides, you will probably never be given the chance to "sell out" that way, but you may be given the chance, have it now in fact, to sell your skill in order to advance a story.

The story is more important than any of us, comrads. The best moments on stage or screen, especially for the actors who manage to keep loving it, come when everyone involved with the production stops looking in the mirror and looks together in the same direction. "The play's the thing," to quote a guy.

What does an actor do for a living?

An actor keeps his instrument in good condition. He doesn't ruin it with drugs, alcohol, junk food, or lack of sleep. If an actor ruins her instrument she soon doesn't act anymore. An actor warms up his instrument so as not to strain the voice or muscles. He increases his performance capabilities through training and exercise.

A professional actor learns to play her instrument like a musician, and plays the song she is paid to play. A professional learns to deliver a performance on time and to the best of his abilities, regardless of personal preferences or personal problems. The professional continually puts in the hours, turning talent into skill, because talent, after all, is only a reservoir of potential, an ability to learn quickly. Effort is required to turn talent into skill, and that means putting in the hours. It means caring. It means loving the craft enough to want to do it for money, and that is a lot of love.

A professional actor continually looks for people to buy his or her skill. Just as a pilot is always looking for a place to land, and a lawyer is always looking for money about to change hands, an actor is always looking for the chance to perform.

A professional actor constantly asks to perform, and constantly lives with the rejection of being told no — time after time. Those days in community theatre will glow warm and notalgic in the mind's memo-

14

ries, but professional actors learn not to take rejection personally. They just move on to the next audition with curiosity and a positive attitude.

A professional actor prepares for auditions by getting all available information about what is called for in the role, and by arriving at the audition with a rested, tuned instrument and carefully made choices to offer the auditors. She "brings something to the table," so to speak, and it may be a revelation to the auditors, something they never thought of. Pros try to arrive early.

If asked to change something in the audition, a good professional actor changes on a dime and offers what is asked for to the best of her abilities. (As Michael Shurtleff points out in his wonderful book *Audition*, this usually means that an actor should add the suggestion to what he or she has already done. Read his book.)

A professional actor uses the good manners his mother tried to teach him and is courteous, though not obsequious or servile, to everyone involved with the project, both at auditions and when he eventually gets work.

Finally, a professional actor does not wait by the phone or strike poses in sidewalk cafes. She gets on the phone, or gets to a desk to write letters or cards. He gets the trade papers and scours them for information about possible work. She gets off her butt and hits the street looking, always looking, perhaps with a bit of a whistle.

A professional actor also occasionally acts.

University Drama Schools
There are about three hundred accredited drama schools in this country. For a list of them, buy the *Directory of Theatre Training Porgrams*. The address is in the appendix. The lady who compiles this excellent directory, as well as several others, is Jill Charles. She's a pro and I highly recommend that you buy her resource books if you are considering going into this business.

A prospective actor should make intelligent choices with regard to university training programs, and with regard to independent acting classes, workshops, and seminars.

It is sad to report that most university training programs for actors still do not train as many actors for the profession as does the School of Hard Knocks. More often drama teachers train potential actors to re-teach their opinions about repertory acting, a profession which

15

does not really exist, much less thrive. It is also sad to report that academic drama departments generally do not feel they have any responisbilty to a student once the student graduates.

Few graduates of drama schools will ever get the opportunity either to teach or to act. We've touched on some of the statisics for actors. The stats for teaching jobs in drama departments are equally grim. As of this writing there is a glut of "acting teachers" with terminal degrees out there looking for jobs. As a case in point, a friend of mine with an M.F.A. recently applied for a teaching position in the drama department of a rather small school in the Southeast. The job description specified that applicants should have either an M.F.A. in acting or a Ph.D in theater. My poor friend did not even make the final cut of applicants being considered. The little school had received applications from more than two hundred people who presumably had either an M.F.A. or a Ph.D. Among these applicants, those that had tried to make a living as actors had probably failed in that endeavor because, though they may have been taught how to act, they had not been taught how to hustle, and had left their drama schools on a children's crusade. Unfortunately this whole situation probably will not change for some time to come.

Let me describe two types of college drama departments which actors, disillusioned with their training, often complain about once they have hit the streets. One might lable these two types of drama department the *monastery* and the *romper room*.

At the monastery the faculty members are stern and severe. Sometimes they are rude and abusive to their students, whereas the powers-that-be in show business rarely are. (In the business they are nice and polite to the actors they want, and simply ignore the actors they don't.)

Drama teachers at the monastery pontificate about art and rail against crass commercialism. Many have a lingering love of British accents and a fetish for silk. (The women generally wear it around their heads, the men around their necks.) Let's call these folks "shouldabeens" in deference to their opinions about themselves. For the most part what they say about art is valuable, but artists like Shakespeare and Moliere would not share their opinion that real art cannot be brought successfully to the marketplace. Since these monastic types refuse to teach their students anything about marketing, they are like generals who send their soldiers into battle without ammunition.

The teachers at these monasteries, though, perform two important services to the industry and to the actors they send into it: They do trim actors' egos down to size, and they do teach actors to put themselves into the service of the work.

And the romper rooms? There, the students' tuition buys their teacher's love.

A musician or an opera singer would never try to substitute "just feeling it" for years of practice to acquire at least a minimum skill, but America is full of actors and acting teachers who seem to think that just being themselves and "feeling it" is enough to do a good acting job. From time to time, though, that one in a million shot proves to be true, like the lottery, and someone who can't act becomes a star, thereby encouraging thousands of other fools to clutter up the business. The romper room schools encourage this kind of folly. They begin with the silly assumption that if an actor will only relax and be honest, then what he or she does on stage or film will be wonderful.

They teach lots of relaxation exercises at romper room. Acting students prowl around the room like angry alley cats, or twitch on the floor like sizzling strips of bacon. This is to unleash the actor's inner creativity, you see. Movement classes often look as though a group of the trustees from the funny farm had been given happy-drugs, bouncing about, skipping along and flailing their arms in the air. This is to "unblock" the students, you see. At romper room you hear people say things like "Brian had a breakthrough today. He cried!" When an actor gushes with emotion in class, the instructor often beams, whether the emotion advances the story or not. The actor is "getting in touch with his feelings." Finally, the graduates are given a final hug (they have previously been given lots of hugs) and told to believe in themselves as they leave for Gotham and Tinsel Town.

Graduates of these schools should immediately get jobs in summer camps or with the Parks and Recreation Service teaching creative dramatics to children. Only a tiny percentage will ever work as actors. But their teachers will continue smiling, beaming, hugging, and drawing their salaries.

In all fairness it should be remembered that theater departments are not very different from other departments in a university. No chemistry teacher can be expected to get all his chemistry majors jobs at

Dupont, and a B.A. in theater is just another liberal arts degree, nothing more. However, many graduates of so-called professional training programs, whether B.F.A. or M.F.A.programs, seem quite bitter about not having been adequately prepared for entry into the profession. They have been given neither a realistic overview of the profession and how it works in real life, nor have they been give specifics on how to beome practicing professionals themselves.

My advice to anyone wishing to go into this business after college would be to double major in theater and anything else. I would advise taking the kind of theatre classes, whether in college or privately, which stress technique and story analysis. You can get in touch with yourself and your feelings as just a part of your homework. I believe that classical training is still the best. Learn to do Shakespeare in iambic pentameter and film acting will be easy.

By the way, don't let anyone tell you that film and stage acting are totally different. They are not. The creative process is exactly the same. It is the delivery which is different, just as speaking to someone at the dinner table is different from speaking to someone across the room. In film acting you usually talk as if the person were standing next to you, and in stage acting you always talk as if the person were across the stage, even in a love embrace.

The stage is where you learn to act, and that is the only place where you really learn to act. You make money acting in film and TV, and that is probably the only place you will ever make much money acting. But first you have to learn to act, so take classes that teach technique, do as much stage work as possible, and get in touch with your feelings on your own time.

Classes which teach you story analysis will help both your acting and your auditioning. Story analysis helps an actor make good, clear choices about what is actually going on in a scene. Once an actor decides on the actions which are taking place, he will be able to advance the story.

There is a clear and rather simple way to do this, and that is to "play verbs," a technique which will be covered in the chapter on "Developing Your Craft in Community Theatre."

If you study drama in an academic setting, it would also be an excellent idea to take at least one marketing course over in the business school, if you can.

You can also find many fine books on marketing at your public library which will supplement what you are learning from this one. In the meantime, finish reading this book. Then instead of lending it to your friends, tell them to buy it. I am a professional and I wrote it so I could make money.

Workshops and Seminars

Picking a workshop or deciding to attend a seminar is not as risky as choosing a college. Workshops and seminars are much cheaper and take less of your time, and they are easier to evaluate in terms of effectiveness. There are many respected independent acting schools, such as H.B. Studios and The Actor' Studio. But you still need to be careful, folks. There are lots of people out there waiting to separate you from your money, including some actors whose names you might recognize.

Let's take a stroll through this territory, and while we're at it let's lighten our load by getting rid of a couple of widespread misconceptions. The first of these is that a person whose face you have seen or whose name you have heard will automatically have something valuable to teach you. (Does Pee Wee Herman teach? He might, for all I know.)

The second is that such a person might be able to get you a job if you go to his seminar or take his class. Some of the 80% of American actors who make less than $5,000 a year acting spend more money under these false assumptions than they make acting.

You may have seen ads for seminars in your hometown paper, where for only $150.00 you can spend four hours with a fellow actor who has actually been on a soap opera! When attractive females give these seminars they often print a photo of themselves in the ad, as if to say "See how pretty I am? I must be right!" and this kind of thing seems to be effective in getting people to spend their money. Wannabees plunk down their cash and leave such seminars as happily innocent as when they arrived.

Before paying for any class or seminar, try to talk to some people who have taken it, and insist that a syllabus of exactly what will be covered be sent to you before agreeing to spend a cent. If the material is not then covered to your satisfaction, demand your money back at the first opportunity and threaten to call the cops if you get any flak. Remember that you are paying for real information! Remember also

19

that people who give seminars and classes do not hire actors.

Due to past abuses on the part of agents, the Screen Actors Guild will not allow a franchised agent to charge for acting classes. Modeling agencies, like the ones in your home town, usually make most of their money by giving classes rather then by getting people work, and so do many small, non-franchised "agents." Please don't waste your money.

There is another kind of "workshop" given by casting directors in New York and L.A. that as of this writing is still tolerated by the unions. Some actors claim to have gotten work through them. You will need to decide for yourself whether you want to spend your money on them. Here's how they work:

Someone reserves a room and asks a casting director if she wants to make $300 for three hours work teaching a "cold reading workshop." If the casting director agrees, a room is rented for $50 and the "workshop" is advertised at $25 a person. Thirty people are "admitted" and after expenses the promoter makes about $350.00.

The actors arrive for the "workshop", and the casting director breezes in a little late. Each actor is interviewed briefly by the casting director and is given a partner and a scene to read from a project the casting director has previously worked on. Scene-partners go out to the parking lot and practice their scenes while the casting director takes a break. The actors return and the scenes are read. The casting director offers some feedback after each one, but since the casting director may never have taken an acting class such feedback may not be much real help. Still, you can learn lots of tricks by watching other actors work, and you do get seen by the casting director.

If you were to go to a "workshop" with a different casting director in L.A. every night, assuming you could, it would take you almost a year and about $7,000 of your money to meet all of them. Many actors think these workshops are worth it. You make the call. If you stay in touch with the casting director, you may get some work out of this kind of workshop, but let's be clear about what this has really been about: You have paid for an audition.

Developing Your Craft in a Community Theatre

Acting is not so much about becoming a character as it is about figuring out and doing what a character would do in a given situation.

Acting is not being. Acting is taking action.

You can not act convincingly by playing qualities such as nice, or shy, or snobbish, or bitchy. To do this is to give, or to "present," your opinion of a character to the audience. This is known as commenting on the character, and when you try to do this you separate yourself from the character and it shows.

By representing a character, however, and doing what he or she would do in a given situation, you wind up feeling as he or she might feel, not to mention advancing the story much more believably. This, in a nutshell, is the difference between presentational acting and representational acting.

Now, let me tell you a story which illustrates the two main approaches to representational acting. Laurence Olivier was on a talk show promoting *Marathon Man*, which he had just completed with Dustin Hoffman. Olivier said that one morning Hoffman showed up looking awful. He had apparently stayed awake for three days in order to look tired in the scene they were shooting that morning. Olivier asked him "Dear boy, why don't you try acting? It's much easier." This is the difference between an inside-out approach to acting (Hoffman's) and an outside-in approach (Olivier's.) Now, Hoffman is certainly a wonderful actor, some say a better film actor than Olivier was, but he is also a star. At this point in your career there just isn't time for you to live the part in order to say a few lines as a day-player.

The American practice of living the part rather than practicing the craft is the result, I believe, of a misinterpretation by Lee Strasburg about Stanislavky's "method." I have heard Strasburg quoted as saying "Stanislavky doesn't know what he means; I know what Stanislavsky means." However, I was not there for that conversation.

Since Stanislavky could presume classical training in most of his actors, he may have developed his "method" to breath new life into techniques which had become two-dimensional and glib. I personally doubt that he ever meant to eliminate technique.

Stanislavky's "methods," such as sense memory, can enhance technique but not replace it, and passion will never be as clear or reliable a means of advancing a story as the making of conscious, intelligent choices about what the character is doing. For me the best acting seems to be a blend of both passion and craft, and is exemplified in the work of such actors as Meryl Streep.

Now, let's take a look at a quick, sure way of advancing the story using the technique of *playing verbs*.

Qualities, like shy or bitchy, are only clues to what a character will do in a given situation. Remember that characters in a story are not necessarily what they say they are. They are what they do—and that includes what they say and what they wish to accomplish by saying it. Isn't this also true of each of us in every moment of our lives? What characters *do* determines what goes on in a story. These actions are best described with verbs, and actors who have learned to play verbs advance the story without causing distractions.

Here's an example of the difference between trying to play a quality and actually playing a verb:

How would you play "reasonable?" Put on glasses and speak with mellow tones? What does a reasonable character do to get what he wants? Persuade, perhaps? Isn't it easier to take action, to persuade, rather than parade around with a character's so-called qualities? And doesn't the action of persuading advance the story much better than someone showing off how well he can play a reasonable man? And don't you already know how to persuade?

Here is a list of some verbs you can use in different story situations, things people really do in interacting with each other.

accuse, advise, acquiesce, admit, affirm
blame, brag,
comfort, challenge, coax, command, criticize, confide,
defend, denounce, deduce
emphasize, encourage, entice
fret, fib
goad, grieve
humiliate
intimidate, inquire
judge, justify
kill
lure
mock, mollify
nag
order, object, oppose
plead, persuade, pardon, pacify
quibble, question

retaliate, retreat, rectify
sweet-talk, surrender, shame
tantalize, tempt, threaten, test
underscore
verify
warn

Practice taking a line from a script and using one of these verbs to invest the line with meaning. Then use a different verb to give the line a different meaning. For example, use the line "The president's plane leaves in an hour" to threaten another character, then to persuade, then to entice, then to plead. (These four verbs, by the way, can be used in hundreds of situations since they are the most common ways we all use to get what we want.) In a rehearsal or an audition, you should always be up to something, and if asked what you are doing, you should be able to answer "I'm trying to _____. Fill that blank with an active verb and a direct object. The direct object will usually be another character in the story. "I'm trying to threaten Henry," or "I'm tryng to seduce John." Practice until you can take a line from a script and say it many different ways by using different verbs. When you are able to do this, you will have developed a basic, marketable technique.

II

The State of the Business

The seven major motion picture studios are Columbia, Disney, 20th Century- Fox, MGM-UA, Paramount, Warner Bros, and Universal. For a fascinating account of the early days of Hollywood, there is an emminently readable book called *An Empire of Their Own*, by Neal Gabler. It tells the "only in America" story of studios and fortunes built by first or second generation Eastern European Jews who began as nickelodeon owners, became distributors, and finally movie producers. They moved to L.A. to take advantage of the weather, which was ideal for filming, and also to get away from Thomas Edison's thugs, who could easily be talked into smashing other people's movie cameras for a dollar or so.

The moguls are all gone now, but Yiddish is still a kind of second language of Hollywood and people use it without even realizing it. The Italian financier Carlo Paretti is reputed once to have made the offhand remark that he was having trouble buying MGM because "the Jews are ganging up on me." *Variety* printed the remark, as well as the responses of several powers in the industry. One response quoted in *Variety* was: "If he said it, he's dead"— figuritively speaking, one assumes.

For some excellent accounts of modern day Hollywood, I suggest *Adventures in the Screen Trade*, by William Goldman, and *Reel Power*, by Mark Litwak.

These days the studios are owned by parent corporations who own controlling interests in the studios' stock and hire intermediaries to keep artistic temperaments in harmony with the bottom line, which of course is profits. The film industry itself has always had its ups and downs, but the studios have managed to keep control of the box office even after the moguls have long since gone. Approximately 95% of the money taken in at the domestic box office still goes to studio pictures. Here's a bit of recent history.

In 1948, the studios finally knuckled under to the anti-trust division of the justice department and sold off their movie theaters. Until that time the moguls had kept thousands of people under contract on their lots and had turned out an unending stream of product to be shown at theaters which they also owned. The only limitation to the studios' aggregate output was the public's willingness to leave their homes and pay to sit in a dark room full of strangers to watch a movie. When the studio-owned theaters were sold, however, the studios not only had to convince people to leave their homes, which became even harder with the advent of TV; they also had to convince the new theater owners to show the movies they were making. Distribution became the key to profits. A product of the highest quality was worthless unless it could be sold.

As parent corporations gained control of the studios, operating expenses were cut to the bone. The contract system gave way to a system whereby the studios use their solid assets — real estate, capital equipment, and film libraries — to generate income. They sell the television and other ancillary rights to the movies they own, use their real estate as collateral to finance independent productions, and then rent their capital equipment to the independent producers they agree to back financially. They also retain the right to distribute the independent producer's product. Mark Litwak has aptly pointed out that most of these so-called independent producers are nothing of the kind. They are dependent producers. A truly independent producer makes a film with his own money, and perhaps then makes a deal with the studio to distribute it, either with a percentage deal or by selling the negative to the studio outright. Such a deal is referred to as a "negative pickup" and is the route whereby an independent producer maintains the maximum financial and artistic control over his film. Few producers have the money to go that route.

When a studio agrees to "make" a picture, they borrow the $22 million or so from a bank at prime rate, and then lend it to the producer at two points above prime to make the movie. The producer must also agree to change the script, hire certain stars, rent studio trucks, cameras, sound stages etc., put studio executives on the payroll to come to the set to hassle the director, and so on.

The studio also gets the right to distribute the picture. The numbers work like this: An average studio backed picture costs about $22 million to get into the can, and another $10 million or so to make copies of the film (prints) and buy advertising, for a total cost of $32 million. The theater owner (exhibitor) gets half the ticket receipts and reportedly steals a bit more. (Remember that time they collected your ticket instead of tearing it in half? They might have sold that ticket again and kept the cash.) So if the entire population of the State of New York goes to see the picture and it grosses $96 million, the exhibitor keeps (at least) $48 million, and returns $48 million to the studio distributor. The distributor takes a third, or $16 million for their distribution services. The producer is left with $32 million. After paying for prints and ads, and then taking the remaining $22 million to repay the money used to pay the studios for equipment rental etc., the independent producer is left with nothing except the salary he received up front. This is why everyone wants his money up front. Net profit points are considered worthless because, according to studio accounting, a picture almost never gets into profit. Yet the studio executives keep buying bigger houses.

Some producers continue to search passionately for what the American audience wants in a movie. Some settle for the knowledge of what the American audience is willing to eat. Both types are pretty good at what they do. A few beautiful movies do get made, as well as a good deal of junk that the public seems happy enough to consume. In addition to taking in 95% of the domestic box office dollars, studio distributed pictures are this country's third largest export, right behind weapons and agricultural products.

Many American mothers have tried preparing gourmet meals for their families, only to learn that their families preferred hamburgers, so it shouldn't be surprizing that many producers become disillusioned and cynical about putting a lot of care into their product. It is not reasonable to expect the studios to have higher aesthetics than their audiences. If your film history professor disagrees, let him go make a movie instead of striking his own kind of poses from his little lectern.

The American Audience
Americans consume more goods and services than the entire Common Market and Japan put together, so it is not surprising that Americans

27

also consume more motion picture entertainment as well. The end-users of the products produced by the film industry—including the services produced by actors—are the people watching the movies. The end-users determine which movies are hits and which actors become stars. Despite all the demographic studies and the millions of man-hours expended by development-types, nobody knows anything for sure. The best the studios can do is to make educated guesses about what the American people want. H.L. Mencken may have been right when he said that "no one ever went broke overestimating the vulgarity of the American people," but in fairness to ourselves we might add that no one gets really rich overestimating our vulgarity either.

About half the people who go to movies are between the ages of 16 and 24, and about half of them are on a date. People over 24 still go to movies, despite their VCR's, because there is just something about that big screen in that darkened theater which takes a person away. Despite the ever-increasing sizes of TV screens, there probably will always be movie theaters.

If a group of guys go to see a movie, they will probably pick an action picture with car chases and things getting blown up. A group of gals usually goes to see a romantic comedy. When a couple goes to see a movie, the one more involved in the relationship will usually acquiesce to what the other wants, as in other aspects of their relationship .

Horror pictures appeal mostly to teenagers. Period pieces and costume epics don't have much appeal to studios because they cost too much to make. This also tends to be true for science fiction, although both kinds of picture still get made.

The word "drama" is anathema to studio execs because they know that most Americans do not go to the movies to have their minds engaged. If a movie forces people to think, they will often leave the theater as resentful as if someone had forced them to run around the block. Consequently they will give the picture bad word of mouth. The word "thriller," however, is considered a very nice word these days.

A buddy picture can be either two men or two women in a comedy or an action picture. Guys will go to see two male stars as buddies in an action picture to see which one is the toughest. Gals will go to see two buddies, male or female, in a comedy to watch the interactions of their relationship. There are obviously exceptions to this, and plenty of them. Generalizations are only generally true.

28

There are also art films that get made. These pictures get seen by only a tiny minority of the population. They engage the mind and give the intellectuals that see them something to discuss after the movie. If you go to see one of these films with an intellectual, and afterwards he asks you what you thought of the movie, you can always say "It was such a deeply moving and personal experience for me that I would prefer not to talk about it."

Sometimes an art film will become a commercial success if it wins a couple of prizes and gets some publicity. Regular people may then go to see it, believing they can achieve some sort of status by going, but this doesn't happen very often, and I say so with regret. Personally, I prefer films which engage my mind as well as my emotions, though that does not mean that I automatically like foreign films.

Foreign films often have government financial help given in the name of art, thus permitting the enormous self-indulgence of some foreign film makers, who seem to be enamoured with myriad camera angles which communicate no new information, and symbols which do not advance a story but turn the story into a crossword puzzle.

When a picture has been filmed, edited and is in the can, the studio will still not release it until marketing studies have shown that it will appeal to movie-goers.

Here's what happens. There are companies, such as The National Research Group in Hollywood, which specialize in determining audience reaction to movies before they get released. This gives the studio the chance to fix something before it is too late. NRG hires people (such as unemployed actors) to recruit members of the public who are not connected in any way with the film industry to go to a screening of a picture before it is released. These recruiters go to a supermarket parking lot or to a shopping mall, anyplace where there are lots of people, and ask folks if they'd like two free movie tickets. There is usually a demographic breakdown that has to be adhered to—so many young teens, so many 16-24 years old, so many in their 30s etc. As I've said, no one connected with the film industry is supposed to be invited to these screenings. The studios know that they can get all the "expert" advice they care to listen to anytime. What they want to know is what the public thinks. Similarly, before General Motors puts a new car on the market, they commission a poll through Gallup or Louis Harris to determine what the public's reaction to it will be. They do not question car dealers. So the studio recruits members of the public for their screenings.

The night of the screening, the recruited viewers arrive at the theater and are questioned again about any affiliation they might have with the movies before being allowed to take their seats. The producer of the movie is usually there with two or three retainers. Typically, he is in his 50's, not very tall, suntanned, silver hair slightly over his collar, and wearing an expensive sport jacket with no tie. He is trying to look relaxed as his beady eyes dart about, and his retainers, not at all looking like sycophants in their early 30's, try to look happy. When the recruited audience has been seated, the producer and his retainers take the seats in the back row that have been reserved for them. During the movie, the retainers take notes of all the audience's reactions- laughs, groans, gasps, etc.

When the movie ends and the credits begin to roll, an NRG employee hops onto the stage and asks the audience to please keep their seats for two minutes. At the same time employees are passing out questionnaires which ask the people in the audience specific questions about their reactions to certain scenes, about actor's performances, and most especially about the movie's ending. It is said in the trade that a movie is about what happens in the last ten minutes, because no matter how good the rest of the movie has been, if it ends badly it will get bad word of mouth.

To become a hit, word of mouth must take over from expensive advertising as the way a movie gets publicized. *Fatal Attraction* originally ended with Glen Close's character committing suicide like Madame Butterfly, and making it look like Michael Douglas's character had killed her. This would have been perfectly consistent with Glen Close's character, but the preview audiences hated that ending. Consequently the studio reshot the ending so that motherhood would triumph over the other woman, and the audience loved it. Women dragged their husbands and boyfriends to see the picture, possibly to show men that there is no such thing as free sex. *Fatal Attraction* became a huge hit, feminist objections not withstanding.

Studios may be able to influence the public, as any large corporation can, but a studio can not shove a $30 million dollar product down the public's throat if the public does not want to consume it. The product must be tailored to suit audience tastes. Again, it is not reasonable

30

to expect the studios to have higher aesthetic values than their audiences. Let's look at how they put a product together.

Screenplay Structure

Film production accepts the tastes of its intended audience, and a good screenplay can accept such limitations and thrive within them.

Almost all studio pictures use the format which follows, and so should any budding writer who wants to write a screenplay. You will see this structure in most movies. Since an actor's job is to advance a story, an actor also should know something about story structure, n'est-ce pas?

Movies are typically two hours long. The human posterior begins to protest like a restless child after two hours, and movie makers want the audience to leave happy. Exhibitors prefer movies that are a little shorter than two hours so they can have showings every two hours and still have time to get people in and out and sell them popcorn. (The concession stand actually accounts for almost half the exhibitor's profits.)

Since only a handful of film directors have what is known as "final cut," the final decision on the length of a movie is determined by what the studio tells the editor to do. The editors are almost always told to bring the movie in at a bit under two hours. Yes, some movies are longer, but if you don't bring up *Dances with Wolves*, I won't bring up *Heaven's Gate*.

One page of screenplay usually equals about one minute of screen time, so screenplays are 120 pages long. That is a screenwriter's limitation number one. If the final movie can neatly be cut to 105 minutes to please exhibitors and help sell the movie, it is often cut despite the groans of the stars or the director. The screenwriter's reactions are not even considered.

A screenplay writer, one who works regularly at least, knows that in the first ten pages of a screenplay, three questions must be answered:

1. Who is the protagonist? (This role is played by a movie star.)
2. What kind of world is the protagonist living in?
3. Why should we care?

If the writer knows the answers to these questions, the story will be clear. Let's use *Working Girl* as an example of what I'm talking about.

In the opening minutes of the film we learn that Melanie Griffith's character works in a fast-paced investment firm dominated by men, many of whom don't take women seriously. A guy named Charlie tells Melanie that he has gotten her a job interview. On route to the interview with her potential new boss, she learns that her interview will be taking place on the casting-couch, so she demands to be let out of the car. She gets out, and as she is crossing the street, a passing car splashes mud on her. Since she is blond and vulnerable, rather than tough and dark, we feel sorry for her standing there drenched and humiliated. We begin to care.

The next scene shows her going to work the next morning, and we learn that she is taking speech classes to better herself. Almost unconsciously, we admire her desire to grow. When she arrives at the office, she puts a new message on the electronic message board which reads "Charlie is a slimeball with a tiny little dick," and she has won us completely with her gumption. You bet we care.

Within the next fifteen minutes, the following three questions must be answered if they have not been already answered in the first ten minutes:

1. Who or what is the antagonist?
2. Who will be in the romantic subplot?
3. Who will be in the complicating subplot?

In the case of *Working Girl*, the antagonist will turn out to be Sigourney Weaver, Melanie's new boss. The love interest will be Harrison Ford, who obviously likes her immediately. The complicating subplot involves her boyfriend, who will later remind her that she could leave the cut-throat business world and be "just a housewife" while he runs his tugboat business. This will tie into the action, later, tempting her to give up her dreams.

Twenty five minutes into the movie something must happen which tells the protagonist that he is going to have to rise to the occasion of impending events, that he or she will need to be better, smarter, braver than before. Michael Hauge calls this the "first inciting incident", and Syd Fields calls it "plot point #1." (Their books are listed in the bibliography.) Whatever you choose to call the event, it is rise-to-the-occasion time. In the case of *Working Girl*, this event is Sigorney Weaver's ski accident,, since it places Melanie in the position of having to run the office while the boss is gone.

32

Within five minutes of this occasion, the protagonist must accept the challenge, and his or her goal must be clearly understood by both the characters and the viewers, even even if the latter understand the goal only emotionally. In *Working Girl*, we all know at this point that Melanie's character must prove herself, and this is the end of "act one."

"Act two" is sixty minutes long and consists of the protagonist solving a series of problems of ever increasing difficulty while trying to accomplish his or her goal. These problems can relate to the romance or the subplot as well as to the main goal. Three romance problems, three subplot problems, and six main goal problems are a safe number to keep the action moving. That's an average of one problem every five minutes for the protagonist to solve.

On page eighty-five an event, or the culmination of events, must make the protagonist pause and feel tempted to give up. We must be able to presume this, even if we do not see the protagonist's hesitation. When Sigourney Weaver's character returns to New York, we may presume that Melanie's character pauses before deciding to go through with the deal she has been pursuing behind Sigouncy's back. The decision to go on must happen within the next five minutes, and the protagonist and antagonist then become locked in a collision course, resulting in a climax where the protagonist may fail but almost always succeeds. This climax is often a ten minute battle full of special effects in an action picture such as the James Bond series. In a love story the climax might be a long scene where the boy concludes he just can't live without the girl and so makes a commitment. In *Working Girl*, the climax comes when Sigourney's character storms into the meeting on crutches and denounces Melanie as a fraud who is "only" her assistant. It seems as though the protagonist has failed, but remember that working girl's got spunk! Leaving the meeting, she makes a last-ditch attempt to prove to Mr. Corporate Man that she was the one who conceived of the deal and actually put it together. Her voice has the ring of truth. Corporate Man inquires further, the turth is uncovered, and "working girl" has won after all.

The climax is usually followed by a few minutes of calming resolution which reassures the audience that things are going to be fine. The movie *Working Girl* has a fairly short resolution, which contributes to the impression at the end that Harrison and Melanie are in a bit of a hurry to hop into the sack. After the resolution, the credits roll. Film buffs and people in the industry usually sit through them.

Watch a few studio movies with this structure in mind, and you will see that almost all of them follow it. If you want to sell a screenplay, you'd better follow it too. This explanation of screenplay structure was written as much for actors as for writers, since an actor's job is to advance a story. A good excercise for actors is to watch movies and, rather than say to themselves "Boy, I would have been great in that movie," to ask themselves, "How could I have helped to move that story along?" Answers to that question can be a big help to actors in auditions.

How Studio Movies Get Made

Deal making in Hollywood is no longer done by movie moguls, nor are deals, for the most part, even put together in the studios anymore. The major deals are put together over lunch by agents, especially from the big three talent agencies, which are Creative Artists Agency, William Morris, and International Creative Management.

At this point let me warn aspiring actors not to be foolish and think "Gee, all I have to do is get represented by one of them and I've got it made." Wrong. You've got nothing they need, no matter how wonderful you are, and even if your "connection" gets one of them to accept you for representation, your resume will sit on the bottom of their stacks gathering mold. The reason I am writing about these agencies is to show you how the business works. Getting the right agent for yourself will be covered in another chapter.

These agencies package projects. They take a script by a screenwriter they represent, get stars and a director they represent to agree to do the picture, and then sell the package to a studio, thereby making not only a 10% commission off the fees paid to their clients, but also a packaging fee for putting together the gross deal, pun fully intended. They perhaps may also get an executive producer credit for one of their executives. Michael Ovitz, head of CAA, might have lunch with Michael Eisner, head of Disney, and conclude a $50 million dollar deal in less than an hour, and the first Michael might well return to his office a million dollars richer. (I can't give you exact figures, though, since he just won't return my phone calls.)

Let's take a look at a typical project from conception to packaging, through production, and finally to release in the theaters and the

34

ancillary markets.

The High Concept Idea
The word "high" in "high concept" does not refer to high aesthetics but rather to high marketability. Advertising in the media is too expensive to be continued indefinitely, and sooner or later word-of-mouth advertising must take over the selling of the picture. That means that an ordinary person must be able to describe what a movie is about to another ordinary person, using a description that must not only be easy to understand, but must also have some some sizzle to it and some appeal. For example, John Q. Public might say something like "We saw this great movie that was like a science fiction version of *Jaws*, except that jaws was inside a spaceship." That would be great word of mouth for the movie *Alien*.

High concept ideas are often fish-out-of-water stories like "What if an African prince went to to Harlem to find a wife?" That idea became *Coming to America*. (The courts later determined that Art Buchwald had been the first to submit this idea to Paramount and that Paramount had not paid Art for services rendered when they gave Eddie Murphy story credit for it.)

Here's another one: "What if a kid made a wish to be big, and got his wish, only he was still a kid in a grown-up's body?" That idea became the movie *Big*. Sometimes an ordinary story can become a high concept idea because of the casting. "What if Arnold Schwartzeneggar and Danny DeVito found out they were twins?"

High concept ideas can be expressed and understood in very few words, both by ordinary people and also by studio development executives, who are themselves somewhat ordinary; like the public, they have short attention-spans. These ordinary qualities put the studio execs in much closer touch with the public's taste than does the erudition of your film history teacher, who is probably a malcontent. Their ordinariness gives them a much better intuitive feel for how the studios should invest their money to get the most bang for the buck.

One morning a development-type arrives at his office at one of the big agencies and finds to his delight that one of his "readers," possibly a cute English major right out of college, has read ten screenplays over the weekend and has written coverage on all of them. Coverage entails filling out a form about each screenplay, giving genre, plot out-

35

line, recommendations, and a one sentence summary of what the story is about, which is sometimes called the "log-line."

Since the exec has never been crazy about reading, he usually reads the log-lines for scripts his readers have provided him with and if he likes one of them he will read the whole two paragraphs outlining the plot. If he likes the plot, he might actually read the screenplay, but there is no guarantee of that, and actually no necessity for it. A marketable idea, including a prize winning piece of literature, can always be "fixed" by an established screenwriter for hire. (Would you refuse to bastardize another writer's work if they offered you $50 thousand for three weeks of your time? "All right, all right, $75 thousand.)

When they buy the movie rights to a story, they buy the right to do as they please with it. Sometimes they just want the idea and couldn't care less about the story. I know of one writer who sold a story idea on a 3x5 note card for $55 thousand dollars. The contract he signed, foreswearing all rights in all time-warps on all planets including, but not limited to, the planet Pluto, was more than sixty pages long.

So this morning the exec's nostrils tingle as he reads an idea. He picks up the screenplay and oozes into his boss's office. His boss, who these days may be named Samantha instead of Sammy, asks "So what have you got for me?" and the exec pitches the idea to her. If Samantha's nostrils tingle, she might say "Hmmm, this would be good for Arnold," and take the script down the hall to the agent who handles Arnold.

The agent listens to Samantha's pitch, and if the agent likes the idea of the story, he will probably read the script, since he needs to imagine Arnold saying the lines in order to decide if the script will keep Arnold in the bucks. If the agent thinks the concept will be a winner, Arnold is sent the script. Meanwhile, Samantha has had the script copied and is clicking down another hall.

The Bankable Elements

There are many people in the movie business who think they know everything, but as mentioned earlier, no one in this business really knows anything for sure. In speaking about bankable elements we should remember that anyone's check can bounce. Still, when analyzing the take at the box office, certain patterns seem to emerge.

People generally go to see stars, not stories. Tell a development executive that you have a tragic story about two filthy, homeless people and he will laugh if he's in a good mood, and tell you he's got no time for bullshit if he's in a bad mood. Tell him Meryl Streep and Jack Nicholson want to do the picture and he will put his hand on your neck and call you "baby."

A studio will almost never back a picture without stars attached to it, because they know that when John and Mary Public pick up the paper to see what's playing at the movies, they are going to look for the names of the stars printed above the title of the movie, and then look at the picture in the ad to decide if they want to see those stars in that situation. Americans often expect stars to act like themselves and not stretch very far out of their personas. They will be amused by an idea like "What if Arnold Schwartzeneggar had to pretend he was a kindergarten teacher?" but they don't want to see him play a shy, lonely hairdresser. His fans would actually become very angry if he did, no matter how good his acting job was. If Arnold made a picture like that, some "critic" working for a magazine would probably write an article pronouncing him "not hot."

Americans want to see what their favorite stars would do in certain situations. Just the idea of Jack Nicholson playing the Joker, for instance, was enough to make people want to see *Batman*. Sometimes, the idea of what certain stars would do together becomes intriguing. "How about Arnold and Raquel Welch together?"

Even if a bestseller has been made into a movie, the story still matters less to the public than who is in it. There are no truly bankable elements, but stars are as close as anything comes.

It is said that in Europe the director is a bankable element and is more important than the stars, but, with the exception of Stephen Spielberg, that is just not so. American movies outdraw European movies in Europe, and Europeans go to see American movie stars, though curiously it is not always the same American stars who draw crowds in other parts of the world. Charles Bronson is extremely popular in the third world, and Mickey Rourke is idolized in Japan.

Along with Spielberg, Woody Allen comes close to being a bankable director. This is because he has a following. He makes intelligent movies that appeal to film buffs, intellectuals, and other urbane types. Film buffs all over the world watch Fellini movies, and Bergman movies, and yes, Woody Allen movies, but these directors do not come as close to guaranteeing a packed house as movie stars do.

A director's status and reputation do help a project get the green light, however, because it is the director who must tell the story in pictures, and a bad story will get bad word of mouth, no matter what stars are in it.

Since any actor's job, including a star's, is to advance the story without causing distractions, stars who remember to act professionally help the story and then the story in turn helps them. Not all of them do this, preferring to showcase themselves.

A director who is good at telling a certain genre of story is regarded as a kind of insurance by the studios. Directors get type-cast too, as action-adventure directors, or mystery-thriller directors, or romantic-comedy directors, and studios are reluctant to trust them with $30 million dollars unless they have a proven track record within a genre.

A high concept idea which has been polished into a good story, plus a couple of stars who want to do the picture, plus a director who is good at telling that kind of a story in pictures, are the so-called bankable elements. They may all come in a package from the same agency.

There is one more professional who is as important as any of those already mentioned: the producer. If the movie gets an Oscar for Best Picture, he will be the one to accept the award. This is not the executive producer, mind you, who actually executes nothing.
The difference between the roles of these two individuals is important In order to get an opening credit as executive producer, plus a handsome, up-front fee, all he needs to do is to put stars and a story together, which are the core of any movie deal. It is the producer who accepts the award for best picture because he is the one responsible for bringing the picture in, and to do that he has to do a lot more than lunch.

I have heard movie producers referred to as nothing but glorified personnel managers, but never by anyone who has ever tried to produce a movie. Would you call a ship's captain a personel manager and say that the guy at the helm is in charge of the ship? Not if you've ever been out of sight of land, you wouldn't. The producer, not the director, is the real captain of the ship, and he is the one accountable to the admiralty back at the studio. The guy at the helm, the director, can be sent to pack his duffle bag pretty much at the producer's pleasure.

Marketing the Film

We should look at how films are marketed before we look at how they are produced, since in actual practice films are marketed before they are produced.

For a studio feature film to recover the costs of production and distribution in movie theaters alone, as in the days of the moguls, roughly the equivalent of the entire population of the State of New York would have to pay $6 dollars each to see the movie.

Now, couple those statistics with these: The Motion Picture Association of America gives ratings (G, PG13, R etc.) to more than 600 pictures a year. Divide 600 by 52 weekends, and you can see why most of these pictures, two thirds actually, will never make it into a movie theater, despite the millions of dollars spent to produce them. For all of these pictures to get into the theaters, the theaters would need to book about a dozen new releases each weekend, and there is not a single weekend of the year, including the weekend before Christmas or the first weekend in June, which sees the release of a dozen new pictures. Making a movie is like mining for gold, and most miners fail. Most of the films that get made either sit in the can or go directly into the ancillary markets, which I'll explain in a moment. For a full length feature film to be financially successful, it usually needs to get at least some kind of domestic theatrical release even if it doesn't make a profit there, and it must later make money in the ancillary markets.

Before the studio agrees to back a picture, studio executives must feel that theaters will agree to show it and people will want to see it. Sometimes a market survey is done. In addition to arranging preview screenings, the National Research Group does this kind of thing also, hiring Hollywood flotsam and jetsam to do telephone surveys which ask people if they would like to see a movie with Arnold Schwartzeneggar and Raquel Welch as deaf mute lovers or something.

A couple of industry mavericks, Golan and Globus, have sold pictures in the film markets of Cannes, Milan, and L.A. before shooting a single scene. I've heard a tale that in one instance they contracted Bo Dereck to appear in the nude in their next film, and then invited buyers into their hotel suites at the film markets. They asked "How many of you guys would like to see Bo Dereck naked?" Many chains booked the film based on Bo's agreement to perform in the buff. Golan and Globus then borrowed the money to make the film on the basis of its presales, and the movie *Bolero* got made.

Roger Corman, another industry maverick, got into the film business by buying a bankrupt lumber company. The warehouses were just fine for sound stages, since the lumberyard was in a rural area where there wasn't much noise, and the high ceilings of the warehouses were fine for hanging lights. The warehouses were also full of lumber which Roger used to build sets.

Corman became famous for developing pictures in reverse order. If he liked an idea, he'd have someone design a poster around the idea. The poster wasn't designed to express what was in the movie, because there was no movie yet. The poster was designed and evaluated according to its ability to attract people into the drive-ins, which were his primary market for low budget films at the time. He would then have someone write a story which expressed the poster. He was famous for not reading scripts, and at development meetings would ask things like "This story has plenty of violence — am I right? And plenty of sex?" Roger not only filled a niche in the market. He gave some pretty famous people their starts: Frances Coppola and Jack Nicholson, for instance.

The studios, which are now owned by conservative parent companies, are naturally more conservative in their marketing approach. A guess is made, and that is all it is despite the market surveys and many meetings, of how many people will go to see the movie in the various parts of the country, and what kind of advertising will best bring those people in. A certain number of prints are planned, and ads are placed on TV, radio, and in the newspapers, while publicists get to work generating as much free advertising as they can by helping to generate news stories about the picture and the people in it. Sometimes the marketing people are right in their predictions, and sometimes they are disastrously wrong, but just getting the picture into the theaters can drive all the other markets, and a picture can eventually get into the black through ancillary sales.

After the domestic theatrical release (which includes Canada) the prints are sent into the foreign markets, sometimes with scenes added or deleted. Six months after the domestic release, the film comes out on video, sometimes with a little added advertising. At about the same time it goes into pay-per-view release in hotels, airplanes and cable subscribers with pay-per-view receiving capability.

The film is then aired on the pay channels such as HBO, then finally on network TV. When the film gets to network TV, it is chopped down to 96 minutes, and 24 minutes of commercials are added to round out the two hour time slot.

Notice that with each succeeding release, a person has to make less effort to see the movie. Paying six bucks to sit in a dark room with strangers requires the most effort. Stopping off at the video store requires less. In a hotel, a phone call gets the cost added to your bill. HBO requires that you write them a check once a month for many movies. Network TV hopes you will just turn on the set and not touch that dial.

When a picture is in development, sales to each of these markets is considered, and often presales are possible if the upcoming film has the status of an *event*. Sometimes a film is deemed to have good potential in all markets, but is still not made because other projects are deemed to have greater potential. A studio may decide to release only thirty films in an upcoming year, and thirty more films in development may sit on the shelf, die outright, or go into "turn around," which means someone else buys what has been done so far to try his luck with it.

This kind of thing is called "development hell" and is considered to be even more painful than just declaring bankruptcy after a picture bombs. That's show biz. It's actually a wonder that entertainment is as good as it is.

The Green Light

So one morning a development-type looked at his cute reader's log-lines and liked one of the ideas. He pitched the idea to Samantha, who clicked down the hall to pitch the idea to a couple of agents who handle a couple of stars. Arnold's agent thought that it might be risky for Arnold to play a deaf mute, but had the inspiration that if they gave Arnold some other kind of handicap instead, maybe Arnold would be nominated for best actor. And Raquel could be the one who inspires Arnold to get up out of that wheelchair, after the audience has been made to really feel sorry for him of course, to "come and get it," or something.

Arnold and Raquel, to everyone's great joy, like the story and agree to do the picture. The original screenwriter is paid to go away, and he starts drinking too much. Another screenwriter, who has secretly been drinking too much for years, gives Arnold's character a new handicap and turns the story into a better vehicle for the stars involved.

So a super-agent and a studio-head have lunch, and the studio takes the package. The studio doesn't have to haggle with the stars over salaries, because the super-agent has already gotten numbers from the stars and presents an "above-the-line" number to the studio-head over lunch. The number includes star salaries, script cost, director salaries, packaging fee, etc. Above-the-line personages will usually get an opening credit at the beginning of the film. One of these personages will be the producer, who may be having lunch as well, and his fee will be one of the above-the-line costs.

Below-the-line costs are what it will actually cost to make the movie, including crew salaries, hotels, catering, location rentals, equipment rentals, props, etc. The producer will offset some of these costs with product placement fees charged to companies to use their products in the movie. If Paul Newman drinks a Budweiser in a scene, you can bet that Bud paid handsomely for that. (The makers of M&M's passed on the chance to have E.T. eat their product and quite regretted it when a competitor took the deal and had their sales go up dramatically because of the success of the movie.) Besides product placement deals, a hotel might agree to provide space for the cast and crew, in return for some prominent shots of the hotel in a scene or two. And so on.

Below-the-line costs can be calculated once a shooting schedule is arrived at. Responsibility for scheduling, budgeting, and keeping the project on schedule and within the budget lies with the producer. The producer is the assembler of all the talents that become the small army that makes a Hollywood movie.

Once the project has the green light, the lawyers are brought in to do their work, after which the above-the-line costs must usually be paid whether or not the film ever gets into production. The film will become a paper corporation with assets and liabilities. It will continue to exist on paper as long as there is any money coming in, or fees and royalties going out.

When the project goes into pre-production, the producer's company, which has been hired as a unit, goes into action, and the producer begins hiring the other talents necessary to make the picture. One of the people hired that will get an opening credit is still not eligible for any academy awards. This person is the casting director.

Let us look, actors, at this life-form which will have such an impact on your careers.

Casting Directors

Casting Directors neither cast nor direct. They don't even direct the casting. Casting directors direct the auditioning. This takes a load off the director and allows him to see a few people for the roles being cast instead of a few hundred.

The casting director has no authority to hire anyone for a role, although sometimes the producer and director will accept the recommendation of the casting director and hire an actor for a small role without ever seeing the actor. This usually happens if the director is busy, and the producer and director both have faith in the casting director's professional judgement. There are some heavyweight casting directors like Mike Fenton and Lyn Stalmaster to whom everyone listens—stars and producers alike—but they are rare.

Casting directors have a lot in common with purchasing agents, such as buyers for department stores. One way to look at what casting directors do for a living is to compare them to someone that you might pay to go shopping for you. You give them a shopping list, tell them to visit all the stores, and report back to you on where the best buys are. This may be too much work for one person to do, so the shopper-for-hire may hire an assistant to help her. After working on a few projects, the assistant often feels perfectly qualified to open her own business, and often does so as soon as she can steal a gig from her boss. There is a professional association in Hollywood which is known as the Casting Society of America, and the casting directors who belong to it have been certified as good persons by the other casting directors who belong to it.

Casting directors rely heavily on the agents they have developed relationships with, just as shoppers usually have favorite stores. They know they will get good, honest, personal service there, and have come to trust those stores' products. It's time for a look at how these "retail stores" do business.

Agents

Agents

There is probably more misunderstanding about agents, and what agents do for a living, than there is about any other single group of people associated with the film industry.This misunderstanding is especially prevalent among actors, who naively believe that an agent's first loyalty is to them, and that it is an agents job to get them work. Most actors believe that the best way to get work is to get a good agent, who presumably will act like their door-to-door salesman and be willing to take actors' phone calls at home when actors are having emotional crises. Since violated expectations probably account for more human pain than anything else in life, let us look at some of these false assumptions in order to head these disappointments off at the pass.

Remember that we are *not* talking about agents who work for movie stars. There are less than a hundred movie stars at any given time, and because of their status, movie stars can get all kinds of people to do all kinds of strange things, like taking phone calls at 2 in the morning. Since for every movie star there are about a thousand professional, union actors who do not get treated as nicely, it behooves us to consider a typical agent's relationship to a typical actor.

First of all, an agent does not really work for actors. An agent works more for her real customers, who are agents for producers, also known as casting directors. An agent works with casting directors to furnish actors to producers as the need arises.

The person who buys the product is called a producer. The person who shops for the product is called a casting director. The product is an actor who can play a character. An agency is a retail store which keeps actors on the shelf until a producer wants to rent one. Actors willing to accept agents as retailers rather than expecting them to be door-to-door salesmen will get along more effectively with their agents because they will understand that a retailer's first loyalty must be to the customer in order to stay in business.

If the supplier of a certain product, an actor, gets huffy and difficult, the retailer can usually fill the space on the shelf by the end of the morning. If an agent behaved like most actors wanted her to behave, she would be out of business by the end of the month.

Look at it this way. Suppose you went into a store to buy some perfume for your sweet-sixteen year old niece, and the store owner tried to talk you into buying talcum powder instead. You don't want talcum

44

powder. You want to buy your niece her first bottle of good perfume, and you tell the retailer that, but she continues to argue with you. Finally, she brings out some perfume, and instead of letting you consider each one, she tries to "hard sell" you a certain brand. You would probably leave that store without buying anything and never go back there again. Yet, strangely enough, most actors think this is how an agent should behave when representing them. An actor hungers to say "Look at me! Look at me! Look at me!" and an actor wants his agent to say "Look at him! Look at him! Look at him!" Sorry, guys, that's not the way it works.

What is odd is that, despite the fact that things don't work that way, agents and the Screen Actors Guild maintain a kind of legal fiction that they do. Agents will look an actor right in the eye and say "I'll work very hard for you." This means that the agent believes the actor can be fairly successful at auditions and would be nice to have on the shelf in case a customer asks for that type. The Screen Actors Guild stipulates that an actor may break a contract with an agent if the agent has not gotten her fifteen days work in any ninety day period, as if it were the agent who got the actor work!

Here's what an agent really does for an actor. An agent provides an actor space on the shelf in the store so that customers can see the actor while shopping. A customer can call the Screen Actors Guild and find out which agent represents an actor to learn which store to go to. If asked, the agent will recommend certain "products" to the customer. This will be done privately, as a service to the customer. A retailer will tell her suppliers (actors) that she recommends their products to customers all the time. This isn't true, but the suppliers are placated and continue to sit on the shelf where the retailer wants them. A customer just might want to buy one, perhaps because a better-selling product is temporarily out of stock, i.e. unavailable due to other commitments.

So an agent provides a place for buyers to go to buy an actor's product. HARRY HUNK. NOW AVAILABLE AT SHARK TALENT.

An agent also gets the best price possible for people she represents, because the more she can get for a product, the higher her commission. A union actor can not make below scale, but if she can get double or triple scale for him, her own commission is doubled or tripled.

Agents are good at negotiating contracts. They are good at looking after the small details which actors might not think of, and agents are good at pushing for more perks in the contract as well as more money.

Producers and casting directors usually prefer to haggle with agents rather than with actors over contracts in order to avoid hurting the actor's feelings. With an agent, it's straight business, with no egos or sensibilities muddying the waters. Producers and casting directors also have more confidence in a product represented by an agent, just as we all have more confidence in a watch bought in a store rather than off the street.

An agent is ultimately a necessity to a professional actor in order to enhance her credibility as a professional, both to have a place where shoppers can find her, and to insure that she is given the best possible deal in a contract. But an agent does not really sell the actor nor get the actor work. The actor does that herself.

The Casting Process

In many an actor's daydreams, the casting process goes something like this: The actor, having found an agent who really believes in him, concentrates on the aesthetics of his art while his agent handles the business-end of things. The agent begins beating the bushes for something that is just right for the actor. She learns of a role in a major motion picture that the studio execs have pictured in one way, but which the agent knows would be even better if her client were given the part, or so the daydream goes. She calls the casting director and praises her client's talents and qualities, and sends over the actor's headshot.

The casting director sees those wonderful qualities in the actor's face, looks at his resume and is extremely impressed with his university and regional theater credits. She calls the agent and asks to see the actor at ten o'clock the next morning. The casting director then calls the director and the producer and with breathless excitement implores them to take a look at someone really special. She goes to bed wondering if perhaps she has discovered the next Tom Cruise.

The following morning the actor arrives, delivers his monologues, and knocks everybody out with his passion. They sign him on the spot. He goes out and buys a sports car, then calls up his mother and his drama teacher to tell them the great news.

This kind of dream pervades the acting community. So do assumptions like "If it's meant to happen it will," and "it" will fall in your lap if you just believe in yourself. Nothing could be farther from the truth. Let's look at how the casting process actually works.

When a motion picture or a television show begins crewing up, one of the people hired is the casting director. The director may request a particular casting director for the job, or he may tell the producer that he has no preference. Remember that the lead roles were probably cast even before the director was hired. Most or all of the co-starring roles may also be in place as part of a package assembled either by the studio backing the film, or by one of the big agencies which brought the project to the studio. The casting director's job at this point will be to present the director and/or producer with a few qualified possibilities for each of the smaller roles.

The casting director is given a copy of the script and a list of the roles which have already been cast. She goes through the script and as each character to be cast is introduced in the story, she notes the character's name and description. Screenwriters have learned not to give lengthy descriptions of these characters, since such descriptions are very often ignored. Character descriptions are only suggestions which give a "good read" to the script. The casting director duly notes what is in the script and may ask the director and/or producer for a meeting.

The director and/or producer may take the meeting, or may simply return the phone call. The casting director goes over the description of each of these minor characters and asks for any preferences about casting. Preferences duly noted, the casting director writes up a casting notice describing the roles being cast, and either mails it or phones it in to *The Breakdown Services*. If a movie is being cast regionally, the character descriptions are faxed directly to the agents located in that geographical region, since these agents may not subscribe to this very expensive publication.

Before I go into how *The Breakdown Services* work, I want to give actors what may well be the most important piece of information of their careers. Even though the descriptions of roles being cast may include some adjectives, like friendly or jealous, or may classify the character as a "Gabby Hayes type," in nine out of ten descriptions there will be four criteria used to define the character. Those four criteria are the character's gender, age, ethnic origin, and occupation. The reasons for this will be covered later in the chapter on how to determine type. Back to the casting process.

The Breakdown Services is a publication which comes out at 5:00 a.m., five days a week, and lists who is casting what. Some hungry Hollywood and New York agents actually get up at 5:00 a.m. to see what is being cast. Most, however, read the "Breaks" in their offices with their morning coffee at about 9:00 a.m. Often the stars and the film's genre, such as romantic comedy or thriller, are mentioned with the title of the project, as well as a description of the roles being cast. Casting notices from bona fide producers are accepted free by *The Breakdown Services*, who make their money through advertising and subscription revenue. Supposedly only bona fide agents and managers are allowed to subscribe to this costly publication, though groups of actors have been known to pool their money and have one of their number pose as a manager in order to submit themselves, usually to no avail. If they were worth submitting, an agent probably would have done so.

The agent looks at the name of the project and the name of the casting director. If the agent has a good relationship with the casting director, her pulse quickens. The agent reads the character descriptions and then goes over to the shelves where the headshots are kept.

Agents have their own systems for organizing actors. All agents separate males and females, although kids are sometimes stored together rather than as boys and girls if an agent doesn't do a lot of kid-business. Some agents have separate shelves for different ages or ethnic origins. If the role described in the "Breaks" calls for a Black male, mid-twenties, to play an engineer, the agent is going to look among the Black males in their twenties whom she represents, and decide which look most like engineers. She is not going to say to herself something like "Tom is a fine repertory actor with many credits in regional theater who could easily stretch to do this role." If Tom doesn't look like an engineer, she doesn't send his picture out, unless, and this is important, Tom has achieved some status in the film industry. If Tom has such status, both his agent and the casting director might pause long enough to consider a small stretch for him. The agent might send his picture and also telephone the casting director that she is doing so, and the casting director may or may not be responsive to the idea. The way actors achieve status in the industry is covered in a later chapter. For probably 95% of the actors in Hollywood or anywhere else, however, it is not a realistic hope to be submitted for anything that they do not look right for. Neither a nice personality, nor heavy regional theater credits count for diddlysquat in Tinsel Town, like they do in your home town.

In considering which actors to submit for each role listed in the "Breaks," type is far more important than talent — gender, age, ethnic origin, and occupation, or what it looks like the person "does," being what determines type. Status is probably as important as type because status is equated with quality, a false assumption, of course, but that's show biz and that's how the game is played.

The agent assembles the headshots she is submitting to a casting director, puts them in an envelope, and goes on to the next casting notice. When she has finished going through the notices, she has a messenger deliver the envelopes. This is a daily ritual. During the day, the agent may also get phone calls from people she has done business with in the past who want to use her services again, mainly because she did not waste their time by sending over actors who didn't look the part. She may send headshots to these clients, or may get the okay just to send over the actors. Sometimes she will tell the client that the actor is on a certain page of *The Players Guide*.

By 11:00 AM submissions begin to be delivered to the casting director's office, and the office is soon inundated with them. The casting director takes the envelopes from agents with whom she has a good working relationship and gives the rest of the submissions to her assistants. The assistants are usually instructed to pick out any name actors they recognize, as well as actors who look like the types being cast. Since there may be hundreds of submissions to go through, there simply is not time to give much consideration to any of them. Imagine someone dealing cards in a poker game, and you will have an idea of how quickly the headshots are looked at, comrades. Don't plan on being discovered this way.

Headshots are picked out because the actors in them look the part. Those to be given a second look are put into piles according to roles being cast, after which the casting director continues the culling process until perhaps six actors will be called in to read for each role. The final choices are arranged so that one phone call can be made to each agent, who is told to "Send over Tom, Dick, and Harry tomorrow afternoon at 5:30. Sides (parts of the script)will be ready at the receptionist's desk today at 4:00."

The agent phones each actor requested and may say something

like "Harry, sweetheart, I got you an audition. Pick up the sides at the Big Orange casting office after 4:00 today. I'm counting on you dear." The actor, with visions of Porches that dance in his head, goes over and picks up the "sides." "Sides" are a couple of pages of the script containing some (probably all) the lines the actor will be reading the next day. Perhaps when he sees that the part is tiny he tells himself that they are just testing him for bigger and better things later. That night he may spend hours rehearsing all four of the lines he will be saying the next day.

In L.A., as well as in most regional markets, the actors called in to audition usually show up either dressed to suggest the character, or, occasionally, to suggest with their Gucci loafers that they are actors worthy of future stardom. In New York they audition a little less dressed up.

The actors are called in one by one to read. The casting director may be alone, or with the director and/or producer. She will read the other parts in the scene as neutrally as possible so as not to steal focus from the actor. Each actor will be thanked politely after reading and the next actor will be called in to read. Often a decision is made immediately after all the actors have been seen once, and the decision may be based on something as superficial as the actor's height or hair color. Competence rather than real talent is all that is usually required. Remember that we may be talking about four lines.

If the part is larger than that, there may be call-backs. Two or three of the actors who auditioned for the role will be given another appointment and perhaps a different scene to read, but again the final choice will probably be based on something like "He's better looking than the star. Let's go with the other guy."

The agent is notified by phone that her client is being booked and that the contract is being sent over. The agent calls the actor and may say something like "You got the part, and I want you to know that I really fought for you. The producer wanted to go with another actor but I convinced him you were perfect for this, so don't let me down." Then again, the agent may be an honest one and say "Mary, they're booking you. Good job." Honest agents do, in fact, exist.

It should be apparent that an actor who tries to look like "everytype" in his headshot looks like "no type" and gets no auditions. Since the romantic leads have already been cast, actors whose headshots make them look like romantic leads are ignored, but a guy who looks like a plumber in his headshot will be picked out of the shuffle when the script has a plumber in it.

To give you an idea of how many headshots are sent out as submissions for these casting notices, I should mention that there is an entrepreneur in Hollywood that sells actors back their own headshots. He collects discarded headshots from casting offices, sorts them out and sells them back to the actors for future use. Now there is a guy who discovers actors!

Television

Let's take a look at the business of television. The three major networks — ABC, CBS, and NBC — began full tilt operations after World War II by convincing radio stations to become television stations as well. Radio stations already had much of the needed equipment, such as existing antennae, that could also be used for television technology, as well as an existing corporate infrastructure that could easily accomodate this new business. A salesman selling radio advertising could call on the same clients to sell TV advertising. The business of both radio and television is to sell air-time to advertisers. What makes that air-time valuable is having a lot of potential buyers tuned in to it.

Based on either a market survey and/or the educated hunch of a TV executive, a TV network tells a client, called a sponsor, that a certain number of people are expected to watch a given television program at a given time. The sponsor is offered air time during the program to broadcast its advertising at the rate of so many dollars per thousand people watching. The A.C. Nielson company is in business to calculate how many people actually watch which shows on television, and the contract between a sponsor and a network usually stipulates that the Nielson ratings will be used to decide how much money the sponsor owes the network. One rating point equals something close to a million people watching. (The numbers change periodically.) If the number of people who actually watched the show was less than what the network estimated, the sponsor gets a partial refund. If more watched than estimated, the amount owed stays the same, hence the networks always overestimate.

You can see why ratings are important. They directly affect the income of the networks.

When a feature film is finally shown on television, it has undergone a metamorphosis of sorts. The network rents the right to show the film on TV from whoever owns the film, and then alters the movie for television. This not only means that the nudity is cut and the cussing bleeped out, but also that a two hour movie is cut to ninety-six minutes and twenty four minutes of commercials are inserted. The commercial breaks get longer and longer as the movie progresses, since the audience also becomes more and more hooked into finding out what happens, until finally the merciful announcement comes that there will be no further commercial interruptions, and one watches the last five minutes of the movie in relative peace.

If a movie is produced especially for televison, it is written in six acts with five cliff-hangers which wontonly await commercial insertions.

Episodes for a TV series are written in much the same way, though the material is predictable enough to warrant some other term besides "cliff-hangers." People who watch certain TV shows regularly usually also read the funny papers regularly. They seem to like to see characters they have come to know in various situations. TV shows usually begin with a teaser of some kind, a small event which reminds the audience of why they like the characters on the show, and then this week's situation is introduced. The situation is never the same in a situation comedy, though the characters and the locale usually don't change. The situation, or problem, might be something as simple as the goldfish died or Cosby wants to cook barbeque. Sometimes a secondary problem will also be introduced, such as Cosby's kid has a test the next day.

In a drama, the problem might be that someone got killed and an innocent person got framed, but the cop who is so cool he has never been required to wear a uniform somehow knows the accused is innocent and proves it in the end. TV shows end with the problem solved and the audience reassured that they too will survive even though their lives are even less interesting than the what they have seen on the tube.

At a seminar I co-produced in Los Angeles once, I listened to a TV producer praise the talents of TV writers. I asked her why it was necessary, if the writers were so good, for canned laughter to be added to the show. She said that when she went to the movies she liked to laugh with the audience and so do people watching TV at home, even if the laughter is fake.

Is this true? You make the call.

Televison commercials are tailored to the show's audience. For example, a sitcom about a widower airs on Saturday night when a lot of poor widows are sitting at home alone watching TV, and the sponsor of the show is a brand of cat food, since lots of widows have cats. Most commercials urge us to spend money we don't really have to buy things we don't really need to impress people we don't really like. Because this is America, friends, where at least we know we're free!

Television and televison commercials, however, are where most actors make most of their money, and despite my not-too-subtle mockery of the medium, I will say honestly that there are very few TV jobs or TV commercials that I would not be delighted to do because of the money involved. Matter of fact, I was just on a TV show where the hero has nothing else to do but ride around in a red Mercedes convertible and help girls.

If you go into this business, you, also, will probably be very glad to do televison and TV commercials. There's a knack to doing commercials which is covered in Iris Acker's fine book *The Secrets to Auditioning for Commercials*, so I won't get into those skills here. But I will say something about "commercial types." Most commercial work is gotten by "All American Types," which, I am happy to say, now includes minorities, provided that they look happy and appear to believe in the system. Angry black males with huge afros will not get much commercial work.

Commercials

Even though most TV stations have production as well as broadcast capabilities, sponsors usually hire independent production companies to produce their commercials and then simply rent air-time from the stations to broadcast them. Independent production companies can specialize in the kind of commercial the sponsor wants, whereas TV stations often are not really set up for specialty productions.

Commercials, at least those intended for national release, cost more money to make, minute for minute, than anything else in show business including feature films. The sound will be perfect, the lighting will be perfect - everything will be perfect except the message, which is usually that the key to human happiness can be found in the use of the sponsor's product. Most actors don't seem to mind the fact that the

53

message is a bit of hype because actors also make more money, minute for minute, from commercials than from any other medium in this business. A national commercial that shoots in one day and runs for a year pays an actor more money than a year of good Shakespeare on the stage, eight shows a week. The commercial may be the financial supplement that allows the actor the luxery to do stage work at all. There are separate, as well as joint, SAG and AFTRA contracts for commercials, and just as a sponsor pays advertising rates which are dependent upon the number of people who see the ad, so actors are paid residuals largely according to the number of people who will see them in the commercial.

Don't confuse commercials with print work. There is no union that covers work actors do in newspaper and magazine ads, and as a result individual actors have little power in negotiations with those who produce such ads. I was in a print ad for Cannon copiers with Jack Klugman that was in *Time, Life, U.S. News and World Report,* The *New Yorker*, and *Scientific American*, and received a total of $385.00. (I somehow suspect that Klugman got more, though.) It also took me months of bitching to get paid at all. My friends back home who saw the ad thought I had hit the big time. Tell you what, folks, when I got that check all I hit were the bars.

It is often suggested that actors have a seperate headshot for commercials, one that looks like the actor is full of exuberant enthusiasm for everything, and that is probably good advice. Also, they usually don't want facial hair in commercials. As a rule they like a clean-cut, all-American look, as I mentioned in the last chapter. "All-American" has finally come to include Blacks, Hispanics, and Asians, provided the actor looks like he or she shares middle-class American values. This is also true for industrials, or "corporates" as they are now being called, which will be covered in the next chapter.

If you want to make money doing commercials, and think you might have the kind of look they're after, I'd again suggest reading that excellent little book by Iris Acker: *The Secret To Auditioning For Commercials*. Everything you need to know about that particular kind of acting is covered very well by the lady. The book is listed in the bibliography at end of this one.

Industrials, or Corporates

Industrials, or Corporates

"Industrials" are training films. They are made all over the United States and are usually commissioned by corporations to teach something to a specific audience, usually the corporation's employees. Examples are films which teach employees how to operate equipment, or teach salesmen how to deal with different sales situations. Various branches of government also commision this kind of film, consequently making Washington, D.C. the third largest producer of them after New York and Los Angeles.

Companies have found that it pays to hire professional actors instead of company employees for these films. Using employees as actors produces about the same result as using warehouse clerks to model clothes. "It just don't look right."

Industrials are a good source of bread-and-butter work for actors, even though union rates for training films are lower than for features, commercials or televison. There is also a good deal of non-union production work done by the independent production companies which make industrials, and they are a good place for actors to get started. Usually the atmosphere is informal and friendly, and sometimes the people who run these companies are as young and inexperienced as the actors they are working with.

Video production companies are in most yellow pages. In New York or Los Angeles there are hundreds of independent companies, many of whom keep their own files of pleasant, cooperative actors whom they call directly for work without going through agents or casting directors.

Feature film, televison, commercials, and industrials are the parts of show business where most actors earn the most money for their acting. Each has been looked at from the point of view of what things are like from behind the camera. Actors and those thinking about making acting a career instead of a hobby need to remember that other point of view and see where they, as actors, fit into the larger scheme of things. Actors must also remember that in each of these media, an actor's job remains the same: to advance the story without causing distractions.

Now let's look at the unions.

III

Actor's Unions

There are many misconceptions about what the term "right-to-work" means. One such misconception is that unions have no power in right-to-work States. Another is that a union actor can do non-union work in a right-to-work State. Both these notions are false.

The phrase "right-to-work" refers to Provison 14(b) of the Taft-Hartly Act. This provision leaves it up to each individual State to either permit or prohibit what are known as "closed-shop contracts" in that State. The big union States such as New York and California permit closed-shop contracts, which stipulate that only union people may work on a certain job, whereas in most States such contracts are not permitted. The latter are the right-to-work States and the "right" in "right-to-work" refers to an individual's right to work whether or not he or she wishes to join a union. One effect this law has is that in Los Angeles or New York, for example, if a producer signs a contract with SAG and then hires a non-SAG actor to do a SAG actor's work, he can be fined a thousand bucks by the union and will probably have other hassles as well. In Florida, which is a right-to-work State, the producer can hire union or non-union actors even after signing a union contract, provided non-union actors are given the same benefits as union actors and the personal choice of whether or not they wish to join the union.

Lots of actors get their union cards this way in right-to-work States. Once an actor joins any of the three unions to be discussed in this section, however, he or she may not do non-union work even in a right-to-work State. Get that straight now please. He or she can be kicked out of the union for doing so. Unions have jurisdiction over their membership in all fifty States and U.S. territories. (If a union actor chooses to do non-union work in France or Zimbabwe, that is his business.)

Craig Fincannon of Fincannons and Associates, casting directors located in Wilmington, NC, which is a right-to-work State, puts it very well indeed when he says that film actors in a right-to-work State still have an ethical obligation to join the Screen Actors Guild, because it was the guild which got film actors such nice treatment. You'll see what we mean in the chapters to follow.

There is another widespread misconception that might as well be addressed here and now, although it doesn't directly relate to the right-to-work laws, and that is the misconception that an actor can enroll in some school, declare that he is on "academic leave" from the union, and then do non-union work.

While it is true that a union actor can act in a non-union production which is a formal part of his training, he may not act in a non-union production which is not a part of his training, even though he is enrolled in school The burden of proof is on the actor to prove any such work is a formal part of his training. If you have any questions about any of this, talk to a union representative. Notice that I said a representative and not a secretary.

Actor's Equity Association

AEA, commonly known as Equity, is the oldest of the three actors' unions because the stage is an older medium than film or television. The conditions underwhich stage actors had been working prior to 1912, when the union was founded, resembled the deplorable working conditions which workers everywhere faced. It wasn't until 1933 that a minimum wage for actors was even established. Equity has jurisdiction only over actors working on the stage, and like the stage it is not doing extremely well financially. It pains me to say this because I personally believe that the only place an actor can learn the craft of acting is on the stage. Nevertheless, actors do not go on the stage to earn a living. They do it for other, often nobler reasons, and make a living in the other media of film and TV. An actor who loves the craft, however, hears the call of the boards for as long as that love of the craft is alive. Many dedicated stage actors spend years maintaining a toehold in New York and doing regional theater, living out of suitcases, although most eventually tire of the life.

To get into Equity you either have to get an Equity contract from a producer who wants to hire you instead of an available Equity actor, or you have to come up through the ranks as an Equity Membership Candidate. Producers are allowed to hire a certain number of extras in many Equity productions at non-union rates. The extras get one "point" for every week they rehearse or perform in these Equity productions as Equity Membership Candidates, and when they have fifty points they can join Actor's Equity Association for $800.00, minus the $50 it cost to become a candidate. They can then work on and off Broadway and at regional theaters across the land, provided someone offers them Equity jobs.

No more community theater for them, or for you, once you join. My advice is to wait until the Equity contract comes to you and then decide if you want to join. Meantime, stay on the boards as much as you can, because it's where you are learning to act.

Some AEA locals permit their members to work for free in certain showcase productions. Some do not. Several years ago the members of the L.A. local of AEA, most of whom had come out to L.A. to do film and TV, forced the union to allow them to work virtually for free in those dingy little rat-hole theaters located throughout the city.

These actors wanted to showcase themselves for agents and casting directors. From what I saw on these L.A. stages, for the most part actors who work in these productions would still rather showcase themselves than do good work that cleanly advances the story. This not only makes for pretty poor theater in L.A. but is probably also a waste of time. Very few agents or casting directors attend these rat-hole productions, so why show off? Stage acting should be done for love, paid or unpaid, to keep the tool sharp and to network with other actors. Besides, even if there should happen to be an agent in the audience, you always do better work when you check your ego at the door.

AFTRA

The American Federation of Television and Radio Artists is the youngest of the three actor's unions, television being the newest medium, and some of its members are neither actors nor artists. A weatherman might claim to be an artist but a newsman had better not. Both may be members of AFTRA. AFTRA supposedly has jurisdiction over live broadcasting and recordings put on video or audio tape, although exceptions to this (that are within SAG's jurisdiction) are covered in the next chapter. Merger with the Screen Actor's Guild has been discussed for years now between the leadership of the two unions, but not much has come of it so far.

An actor can join AFTRA by paying a membership fee which varies depending on the local, $800 dollars in L.A. for instance and $400 in Atlanta. Actors who change jurisdictions pay the increase if they work in the new jurisdiction within three years after joining, but not after three years.

AFTRA does not recommend that an actor join the union until the second AFTRA job he or she works. Some other considerations about when to join any of the unions will be covered in the next section of this book, AN ACTOR PREPARES. For now let us just say that since most TV and radio work in regional markets is still non-union, actors working in those markets usually postpone joining until they have a pretty solid resume.

AFTRA membership can be helpful to someone moving to a new market. Many regional offices are shared with SAG and can provide signitory lists and other useful information to members. Also, if an actor works an AFTRA job and remains a member in good standing for one year, she becomes eligible to join SAG, and SAG is where the money is.

The Screen Actors Guild

This one is your money maker.

Expensive TV shows and TV commercials are often shot on film and then transferred to tape, and actors as a rule make more money on expensive projects than on cheaper ones. SAG actors' wages are the highest in the industry.

SAG benefits are also the best in the industry. In any year that a SAG actor makes $12,000 dollars, she gets free medical, dental and life insurance. Any year that he makes at least $5000 in film is counted as a vested year. Ten vested years will get a SAG actor a retirement pension at age sixty-five, as well as reduced earnings requirements for health insurance prior to age sixty-five.

The working conditions for SAG actors are also the best in the industry. Film crews fly tourist class to locations. SAG actors fly first class. Extras swelter or freeze outside on the set while SAG actors relax in their trailers. There are even rules that extras can not eat off the same tables as SAG actors, nor ride in the same vehicles with them.

The Screen Actor's Guild is the most powerful union in Hollywood and its president one of Hollywood's most powerful people. It is said that if the electricians go on strike you can shoot out of town and if the teamsters go on strike you can shoot out of State, but if SAG goes on strike you are shoot out of luck. SAG can shut down a production anywhere in the U.S. while its representatives make the producer jump through hoops while holding his wallet in one hand and his ulcer in the other. Even in right-to-work States Hollywood producers hire SAG actors whenever possible, both to keep the union happy and also because it is usually more cost-effective to pay a SAG actor $504, as of this writing, to say a line of dialogue than to work with someone with little or no experience. An actor who needs ten takes to get the line right uses up a lot of crew-time, and that winds up costing more than paying the SAG actor. Often low-budget pictures using a non-union director and a non-union crew will still sign a SAG contract so they can use SAG actors, even though they are not using any stars. Any picture using stars will have to sign a contract with SAG, since all stars are members of the Screen Actors Guild and prefer to work with experienced, union actors.

SAG's jurisdiction covers all acting work done on film. SAG, rather than AFTRA, also has jurisdiction over industrials since it negotiated industrial contracts before AFTRA existed. This is true even for training films shot on video tape. SAG also has video and audio recording contracts which AFTRA claims are raids into its jurisdiction but which AFTRA is powerless to prevent. SAG contracts are negotiated with producers' representatives every three years and then imposed on everyone else.

Speaking a single word such as "hello" turns an extra into an actor, and the speaker must be given a SAG contract if the producer is a signatory. In States such as California which permit closed-shop contracts, a union actor must be hired to say that word. If a producer wants to hire his daughter to say the line a "bonus" of $1,000 dollars must be payed to the union. The union calls it a fine. The producer calls it a bribe. Under certain circumstances a producer may hire a non-union actor without penalty in a closed-shop State. If there is not an available union actor meeting the discription of a character in the script, an albino midget for instance, the producer can hire a non-union albino

61

midget and the midget gets to join the guild. In a right-to-work State, there is no penalty legally permitted for hiring a non-union actor, but such activity is kept to a minimum. Also, an extra in a closed shop State may be upgraded and given a line if he or she is established in a previous shot and the director decides the actor needs to say a non-scripted line. Reshooting the whole scene in order to use a union actor might cost the producer $100,000 dollars, and SAG concedes this is not reasonable. Once an actor speaks a line in a union picture, he or she may join the guild. The cost is two days pay plus the first six months dues, or $1068 dollars. Yup.

There are other ways to get into the guild. SAG took over jurisdiction of extras when the Screen Extras Guild went belly-up in 1989. Anyone who works three days as an extra on a union picture and makes at least $100 a day is eligible to pay the $1068 and join the guild. Also, anyone who has been a member in good standing of another performer's union such as AEA or AFTRA for one year, and has worked at least one union job during that time, is eligible to join SAG.

This card is your money maker and you can't get an agent in L.A. without it. The time to join will be discussed in Section IV.

IV

An Actor Prepares

When you go into business, any business, you must decide two things: what are you selling and to whom are you trying to sell it. Since a professional actor is someone who acts for money, he or she must also find someone willing to pay him or her to act.

This section is about deciding what to sell and how to set up shop in whatever market you happen to be working. The next section is about finding buyers and doing business. Let us all remember that no one gets a 100% market share. We must each first find our niche somewhere in the marketplace.

An actor may have the skill to make a certain role sound good, but if he doesn't *look* believable in the part, that's a distraction, and that includes being too pretty for the part.

The criteria of sex, age, ethnic origin, and occupation are primary in determining type, precisely because these are the four things which affect the way the world treats a person and the way a person looks at life.

Think about this for a moment. Men and women see life differently, whether the causes be from heredity or from environment, and the world treats the sexes differently. Moreover, male or female, you think differently at twenty than you do at forty, and the world treats you differently. Your ethnic background gives you certain assumptions about life—like it or not—and even though you may have disavowed those assumptions, you have been treated at least in some small degree as a person from that ethnic group.

These first three factors, however, are not as important as the fourth factor, which is occupation.

When you meet someone at a party and begin to have a conversation which leads you to believe that you would like to get to know the person better, you usually don't ask his age, or if he is of Italian or

Greek origin, though you may have a kind of passive curiosity about those questions. Usually you first ask "What do you do?"

In his novel *You Can't Go Home Again*, Thomas Wolfe observed that a person's occupation is by far the most important thing in determining how he views life, more important than a person's nationality or cultural background. A French cop and a German cop, for example, have far more in common that a French cop and a French doctor.

What you "do" means what you do for a living, and we answer the question "What do you do?" with "I am a teacher," or whatever one's occupation happens to be. It shouldn't surprise us, then, that characters in movie and TV scripts almost always do certain things for a living. Rarely is a character in a script described as a passerby. He will be described as a cab driver, or a hot dog vender, or a cop on the beat. The actor cast in that little role may be male or female, black or white, but he or she will look like he or she does that for a living.

Some handsome actor walking the streets of Studio City, hungry and broke, may curse the industry for not letting him say the cab driver's line when he could have said the line just as well as the guy who got the part. (And could also have gotten his beautiful mug on the screen and then possibly have been discovered!) He didn't get the part because he didn't *look* the part.

So how do you determine your type? Well, you do a market survey before you put your product on the market, just like Ford or Disney does.

Ford did not survey car salesmen before introducing the Mustang; they surveyed potential car buyers. (This is how Gallop and Harris make most of their money, by the way, not through political polls.) When a studio previews a picture, it doesn't ask the opinions of critics or cinematographers. In fact, those in charge of the preview will not let people connected in any way with the film industry into the screening. The studio gets the opinions of the end users of the product (the moviegoing audience) just like the Ford Motor Company did, and so should you. Do not ask your drama teacher what type you are, or other actors or directors. Ask John Q. Public. Here's how to do it.

The first thing you do is buy a pack of 3x5 note cards—one hundred is best. Since about half of the people who go to movies and watch prime time TV are between the ages of 16 and 24, take 50, or half your note cards, and put "16-24" in the upper left hand corner of the cards. Then write "male" on 25 of them, and "female" on the other 25. Put a rubber band around each stack. Divide the rest of the cards into five equal stacks and label them "under 16," "late 20's," "30's," "40's," and "50 plus," and further divide each of these categories into "male" and "female." Put a rubber band around each of these little stacks.

You might as well get most of your "16-24" answers on the campus where you go to school if you are a student. If you are not a student, you will probably be asked to leave the campus, and you should do so politely, but you may have filled out a lot of cards before you are asked to do so.

Now go to a place that has a lot of pedestrian traffic, like a shopping mall or a supermarket to get a more complete audience cross-section. If a mall guard hassles you about no solicitation, tell the Neanderthal that you are not soliciting but are doing a research assignment for a class at the university and are almost finished. You might as well smile and ask his opinion of your mug while you've got him there. It might even molify him. Also, the university part will usually intimidate him, but if he doesn't drag his knuckles back to his office and just continues to gape at you, you can go on out to the parking lot. You can work just as well or better out there. If they run you off from there, go someplace else. The more completely you do this survey, the clearer picture you will have as to how a movie-going audince sees you. This will tell you where the door to the acting market opens easiest for you.

As you see a person approaching you, guess his or her age and gender if necessary, then take out a card from the appropriate stack of age and gender. Smile, go up to the person and say something like "Excuse me. I'm doing an assignment for an acting class to determine my type. Would you please guess my age? Your first impression, whatever it is please." Most people will usually go along with answering one question. Yes, this is a lot of smiling. So is the business.

When they have guessed your age, go ahead and ask the really important question: "Just looking at my face, what does it look like I might do for a living—besides act of course." Obviously you should be dressed as neutrally as possible so that your clothes don't lead the witness. Wear something that either a white collar worker or a blue collar worker might wear to the mall. Look as neutral as possible and let your persona ask the questions. If you are a student and people say you look like a student, ask what it looks like you are majoring in, so you can narrow things down.

You will find that most people will give you friendly answers. Some may brush you off, but that in itself will be good training to get you ready for the industry, so learn to take a deep breath, smile, and go on to the next one.

You already know your sex, so you presumably won't have to ask people if you look like a man or a woman. If you do have to ask that, you are going to have a very hard time in this business.

If you really have questions as to how people see you in terms of ethnic origin, save that question for last, since it is more important to get answers to the other two questions. If you want to know how Hispanic or Jewish you look, ask them to guess your ethnic origin after they have guessed your age and occupation. If everyone says you look Jewish you will probably never get cast as a lumberjack, at least not in a paying job. But there are comparatively few roles that are rigid about a character's ethnic origin these days. Still, it doesn't hurt to know it, and you can probably determine it yourself without asking.

The two basic Caucasian subgroups are Northern European and Mediterranean, with Jewish and Hispanic falling into the Mediterranean category. Al Pacino can play a Jew and Andy Garcia can play an Italian without distracting anyone.

If you are Caucasian and time permits, you may want to ask them to guess your ethnic origin. If you are Black or Asian you probably don't need to ask. The American eye is not sophisticated enough to differentiate between Chinese and Japanese, nor between East or West African.

Since we're talking about ethnic origins in casting roles, we should mention that the way the public perceives type was the reason behind the de facto racism that pervaded the entertainment industry until affirmative action began to change things in the sixties.

A black actor would show up at a casting call and be politely told that there were no "colored parts" in the project. He might say that he hadn't come to audition for a "colored part." "I'd like to read for the school teacher. My father's a school teacher. I can do that role."

"I'm sorry," the voice would say. "That's not a colored part."

The reason for this kind of thing was not due to racial hatred on the part of the producers, who were probably liberal democrats for heavens sake, but rather because it was assumed that a black actor in such a role would distract from the story. Beginning in the sixties, the producers and the unions began to take some action to change things. Negative stereotypes were not eliminated by any means, but small roles that could serve as positive role models for minorities started to be given to minorities. A favorite such role these days is the character of color who passes on some information to the protagonist, such as a forensic expert, hmm let's make him an Asian, who says "The cause of death was strangling, not drowning." This kind of affirmative action both reflects a changing society and also encourages the change, thereby bringing realities a little closer to professed ideals.

This market survey to determine your type will take between three and five hours, depending on how many people you choose to question. The way to talley the results is covered next. If you skimp on this survey, however, you may do yourself a great deal of harm. You may waste time clinging to your affectations, which are a form of ego and just get in the way of the work.

Deciding What to Sell
When your survey is complete, tally the results. Here's how. First, average all the ages guessed to arrive at the average or median age that you look to John Q. Public. Then divide all the cards into two stacks—one stack for those who guessed above the median age, and one for those who guessed below the median age. (Those who guessed exactly the median age should be put aside for now.) Average the low stack and then average the high stack, and the resulting numbers will give you your age range. There are probably many wonderful roles within that age range. The median age itself tells you how old you should look in your headshot.

Now that you have your age range, divide the cards into two stacks, one for white collar jobs, and one for blue. The dividing criteria should be whether or not you need a college degree to get the job. One stack will probably be a good deal bigger than the other. List the number of times each occupation is mentioned within the bigger stack. One occupation will probably be guessed more than any other, and in addition to the occupation that was guessed the most, there will probably be other similar jobs that also get a number of votes. These other occupations will suggest your line of characters.

For headshot purposes, go with the occupation that was men-

67

tioned the most, for that is your strongest suit and that will be the easiest way for you to penetrate the market. When you get your pictures done, dress for your headshot as though you were going to a job interview to try to get that job. You can always ask someone with that occupation what would be appropriate to wear.

In the survey I did to determine my type, I came out with a median age of forty and an age range of thirty seven to forty five. The occupation mentioned the most was a teacher, but jobs like psychiatrist, scientist, and architect were also mentioned a lot. My head shot looks like a forty year old professor in a tweed coat. My line of characters consists of educated professionals. This is the product I sell. This is the part of the film market I concentrate on.

General Motors will happily sell a station wagon to a single man but will not spend any advertising dollars trying to do that. I will happily play a mechanic if asked but I'm not going to try to promote myself that way.

If people tell you that you look like a mechanic and you've always wanted to play blue-blooded gentlemen of leisure, then you need to do some serious soul-searching. Do you really want to spend the next five years hustling the kind of roles you are likely to get? Don't kid yourself that they are going to pay you to stretch. If you look like a mechanic but have this emotional need to play blue-blooded gentlemen of leisure, you might consider either doing some politicking in your community theater, or else try producing projects yourself, starring yourself, and, I hate to say it, probably losing your investment.

If, however, you are quite happy to practice your craft playing roles that your market analysis suggests you can get, you are now in a better position to succeed than most actors are, especially if you look like a mechanic or something else not very glamorous. Most actors want to compete for the glamorous roles, and most will fail. By playing non-glamorous roles you might get into the game, earn a small but well deserved reputation within the industry, and in a few years be given a role, glamorous or not, that makes you an overnight success after those years of hard work. Or, you might just have a satisfying, thirty year career as a working actor who plays certain kinds of roles and retires with a nest egg and a pension.

Remember that the basic difference between an amateur and a professional is that a professional does it for money. In deciding whether an attitude or a certain kind of behavior is professional or not, ask yourself the following question: Would anyone pay me to do this?

If your market survey tells you that you look like a certain type, and you have put in enough caring hours to turn your talent into skill and can play the type you look like, you have the ability to get paid to act. You've got something you can sell.

You may be a bit disappointed about the product you have the best chance of marketing. Welcome to the real world. A restauranteur may love his quiche but make his living selling hamburgers. Without his hamburger business he would never sell any quiche at all.

Think of your market survey "type" this way: If Steven Spielburg called you up and asked you to play a plumber or a waitress in his next movie, would you take the job? If you wouldn't, then the luxury of remaining an amateur is yours.

Packaging Your Product

I've mentioned headshots a couple of times. A headshot is an 8x10 black and white picture, usually from the collorbone up, although at this writing there seems to be a bit of movement toward shots which show the actor from the waist up. As an actor you must never leave home without one.

When you are shopping for a product you are often able to find it on the shelf because of the box it is in, a box which is specifically designed to tell you what's inside. That's what your headshot should accomplish.

In a store, sometimes you pick up the box and read the printed information in order to reassure yourself of the product's quality. That's what your resume should accomplish.

Remember to think of a casting director as someone who is paid to go shopping, and to think of a talent agent as someone who helps a shopper in her owner-operated retail store. This should help you to make clear decisions about how to package yourself. You are going into business to sell something specific, and your first marketing goal is for your headshot to change hands between the retailer and the buyer. Later, once you have succeeded in getting into the market and in doing some business, you may be able to diversify and expand your product-line, but your headshot and resume should tell perspective buyers what you can bring to the table, right now, with little or no preparation.

That is the other half of what availability is about - not only can you come to work right now but can you deliver something specific right now. This is what your packaging should tell them.

Headshots That Sell

Here is an area where most actors commit professional suicide, aided and abetted in this by photographers who think that it is their job to make an actor look as young and as pretty as possible, like a romantic lead who just arrived from heaven. This is precisely the segment of the market where there are the fewest roles and, because of the affectations of so many "actors" who want to get into this business, where there is overwhelmingly the most competition. I can give you no better advice than to try to avoid competing in this part of the market.

Take charge of your own headshot session and make sure the photographer understands that it is your career the session is about, not his. If the photographer's attitude is not amenable to working this way, hold up one of your fingers in front of his face — you know which one — and leave. Actually, a phone call beforehand can save you both some time. Tell the photographer that you want to sell something specific with your headshot, the specific type that was determined by your market survey, and that you want the headshot to look so much like you that if you held it next to your face it would represent you exactly. There is nothing that makes a casting director angrier than discovering that an actor called in for an audition does not look like her headshot, and one of these days photographers will understand this. Find out what the photographer charges for 72 shots, a contact sheet, and two different 8x10s. Compare prices in your area, remembering that there is no need to spend a fortune on headshots. A good headshot is one that looks like you.

You hear a lot of nonsense in this business, like there need to be two lovely points of light in each eye or your career is over and blah, blah, blah. Nonsense. Remember the casting process and the poker player dealing cards? Your headshot should look like an honest representation of what you can bring to the table, and that should be an actor who is easy to work with and who is believable as a certain type. No more, no less.

Before you go to your session with the photographer, decide what you are going to wear. A headshot is actually at least a head and shoulders shot, and the collar of the shirt you are wearing in your headshot is going to have an effect on the casting director who sees the picture. If someone tells you anything different, try putting on a couple of contrasting outfits, a necktie and a tee shirt for instance, and compare the two looks. Quite different aren't they? Let your collar suggest your type, and get several opinions on your choice of collar before the shoot.

Now rehearse for the shoot. Look in the mirror and practice giving good news with your eyes. Your eyes are the most important reflection of what is inside you. Mary Lyn Henry, author of *How to be a Working Actor*, says to consider the eyes an extended handshake. I like that.

Michael Shurtleff, author of *Audition*, likes to see a bit of mischief in the eyes, which tells him the actor would be fun to work with. My advice is, if you are a doctor-type, mentally say something with your eyes like "Your child is going to be just fine. She'll be able to go home tomorrow." If you are a mechanic, you might say something like "It was only a loose connection." Look in the mirror and send this information with your eyes. You know your face better than any photographer ever will, and this is another reason to take charge of your shoot. I like to work with a photographer who is willing to set up a mirror behind the camera so that for the first few shots I can look in the mirror and snap my fingers when I want him to take the shot. This shows the photographer what I want to accomplish and helps him to make suggestions of his own. You'll get a lot of good shots this way.

You do not need to pay a professional make-up artist to do you up before the shoot. Are you going to hire a make-up artist before every audition? Do your own make-up and keep it light. If your wrinkles and lines will show when you are interviewed, they should show in your headshot. Those wrinkles could well be what gets you the part. Tell the photographer this.

A few days after the shoot the photographer will give you a contact sheet, which he makes by putting the negatives on top of an 8x10 sheet of photo paper and exposing it. You will need a good magnifying glass to see the results. They sell a thing called a "loupe" in photography stores for a couple of bucks which is designed for this purpose. Again, get several opinions about which two shots best sell your type — not which ones make you the sexiest — and then order those two from the photographer. Get several opinions again about which of these two photos best sells your type and choose that one to be reproduced.

Photographers and actors have different self-interests. He may try to sell you 3x5s at an exorbitant rate instead of a contact sheet. He will probably insist on keeping the negatives, and may try to sell you several 8x10s at prices ranging from five to 15 bucks each, or tell you that you haven't a chance of success unless you hire him to shoot an expensive composite for you. Don't buy any of it. Get a good price on 72 shots, taken as per your instructions, with a contact sheet and two 8x10s included. Then pick one 8x10 and have it duplicated yourself. You do this by sending the 8x10 to one of the photo duplicating companies listed in the index. Personally, I recommend Photoscan in Orlando, Florida. As of this writing, you get two hundred 8x10s for 69 bucks.

Until recently, professionalism dictated that your headshot be cropped from your collarbone to just over the top of your head and also that it be borderless, or bleed-cut. In other words, it should have no white frame around it. Even though there seems to be some flexibility about this at present, the above format will work anywhere and is the safest. Your headshot should have your name printed on the front in letters big enough to be seen from across the room. A white strip along the very bottom with your name printed on it works just fine and is sometimes easier to have done than having your name printed across your shoulder in contrasting letters. Many actors have their union affiliations printed under their names. I am not convinced this is necessary.

You can not go into this business without an 8x10 headshot that tells people what you are selling. Until you have headshots you are an amateur. Period. To get started in this business, first do your market survey, then get your headshot taken, and then have one shot duplicated. While you are waiting to get your prints back, put your resume together.

The Resume

Your resume will be stapled to the back of your headshot. Your photo describes your product with a picture, and your resume describes your product with words. A resume should be factual and business-like and say that you are capable of delivering a useful product. If you stick to the format recommended by the Casting Society of America your resume will seem more professional. I have included a copy of my own resume at the end of this book for you to refer to.

Across the top, again in letters big enough to be seen from across the room, goes your name. Keep it simple and write it the way you would introduce yourself. Would you introduce yourself to a casting director as Hatcher Thatcher Baxter the third? If you think she would not be greatly impressed by this introduction and you would introduce yourself to her in your usual way as Hatch Baxter, then print that on your resume. When you sign a contract you can specify that Hatcher Thatcher Baxter III be put in the credits if you want, but you'll probably get over that after a while and reserve that name for your signature. While we are on the subject of names you should know that you may not be able to use your own name if someone else in the union under whose jurisdiction you will be working is already using that name. A phone call to the appropriate union will tell you if your name is still available.

Under your name, put your union affiliations. This information must go on your resume whether or not you print such information on your headshot. If you don't list a union it is assumed you are not a member, and it is very rare for an agent to bother sending a non-union actor to audition for a union job. Remember that union jobs are where the money is.

On the left side of the resume, underneath your name and union affiliations, put your vital statistics of height, weight, hair color and eye color. That's all. Your headshot should reveal your age range, and clothes sizes are for modeling composites.

On the right side of the resume put either your home phone number or that of your answering service. There is no need to put your address and some reasons not to, especially if you are a female. You'll be sending out a lot of these photo/resumes and most of them will wind up in the dumpster. Somebody sleeping in the dumpster one night might find your headshot, fall in love with you, and decide to come over to tell you so.

As soon as you get an agent, the agent will give you a sticker with the agent's address and phone number. Paste this over your own phone number, make photocopies, and attach these copies to your headshots. Next, list your acting experience. Some actors stretch the truth, but I think this is a bad idea. The longer you stay in the business the smaller the business becomes. If you get caught in a lie your believability suffers, and an actor needs, above all, to be believable. However, even though this may seem to contradict what I have just said, I think you should have two resumes, one to make stage folks think that the stage is your main interest, and another to make film and TV folks think you have only been doing stage work to practice for film. In other words, have one resume which lists your stage credits first and another resume which lists either film or TV credits first. If you have more TV credits than film, list TV first and vice versa.

For stage credits list the name of the play in the first column, then the name of the character you played, then the name of the theater where the play was done, or the name of the director. To have worked at the same theatre twice says something good about you.

Film and TV credits list the name of the film or TV show, but not the character's name. The thinking here is that casting directors can not be expected to have seen everything that has been produced or to remember every character's name. They want to know how big the role was. "Featured" means a day-player. A weekly contract usually gets you "co-star" status. "Recurring role," "guest star," and "starring role" are the other categories. Do not list extra work at all, not even to fill up all that dreadful space. It only makes you look like a beginner that doesn't know any better.

You never list your commercial credits. You put "Lists and conflicts available upon request." If you put down that you did a Coke commercial it can prevent you from getting one for Pepsi, even if the Coke commercial is no longer running. (If it is running, or if any commercials you have done are still running, you can not do any conflicting commercials. To do so will get you fined by the union and sued by the sponsor.)

Industrials, also called "corporates" or "training films", may be listed if they are all you have for the moment. The first column should list the name of the company that commissioned the film, the second the occupation rather than the name of the character you played, and the third column the name of the production company that made the film. Eventually under "Industrials" you will put "Lists upon request," like you do for commercials.

Next you list the training you have had that is relevant to the acting profession. A course in Tantric Yoga is not relevant. A BA in theater is relevant, but not as relevant as the workshops you take with professionals. The proliferation of theater degrees has watered down their meaning unless the degree is from someplace like Juilliard. The purpose of training is to reassure people in the business that you have at least some idea about what you are doing, and the very fact that you continue to take workshops gives them confidence in you.

Next you list any special skills you have. Do not list things like "Good with children and animals." List all sports you look good at while you're playing them, as well as any kind of mechanical equipment you can operate. These things can get you a lot of work in commercials and training films. If you list a skill, make sure it is something you can do well, right now, not something you think you'd like to learn. Learn how to do them on your own time and then list them.

Remember that your resume is a professional declaration of your abilities. If you are not a fly-by-night scam operation, if you plan to be in business for years, it is easier and much more practical to be honest every step of the way. Growth takes time. Eventually all that empty space on your resume will be covered with your real achievements. If you don't have much to put on the resume yet, say so honestly in a short biography of yourself and let the bio suggest your type and professional attitude. Remember that, at one time, everyone you have ever heard of has had a blank resume.

Promotional Materials

Promotional materials are advertisements for yourself. If you believe that your small acting business doesn't need to advertise, that if "it" is meant to happen for you then "it" will, your business is almost certainly going to fail.

Again, most actors would rather hold on to their affectations even if to do so means not working, and many of you will read the above paragraph, feel vaguely troubled by it for awhile, and then ignore it. Your business will go under, probably within three years, while those of you who pay heed will struggle and stay afloat. The choice is yours.

Advertising has one purpose, and one purpose only, and that purpose is to increase sales. When you advertise, you want to get the most bang for the buck. There is no point in spending money to advertise your product to people who will never buy it. Thus an ad in your hometown paper is largely a waste of money, whereas an ad in one of the trade papers is more focused and a better investment. Still, I don't recommend spending money on those ads either. It is not cost effective and actually seems a bit tacky. Perhaps some actors have gotten work by printing their mugs in *Variety*, but I have never met one. Up and coming stars sometimes have their pictures in there, and if you get to be one of those, then consult with your agent and/or manager about what the best course of action is. For the beginning actor there is no substitute for leg work and direct mail advertising. In spite of the fact that casting directors are bombarded with them, postcards with your picture give you the most bang for the buck. The same places that duplicate headshots will also print postcards for you, usually in lots of a thousand.

Casting directors are divided in their opinions as to the usefulness of postcards, but the bottom line is that they never hurt and they can sometimes help. I advise using them, definitely in local markets, but also in the big-time. A postcard once a month to anyone who can give you a job will eventually pay off simply because of the percentages. Besides, postcards will cost less than a third as much as mailing out headshots.

You can also use postcards in other ways. You can use them as oversized business cards, as a kind of personalized stationary for "Thank You" notes after auditions, or as personal notes for use with a flyer about a play you are in, or with a photocopied review of your work. While it is true that some casting directors throw postcards away without reading them, if you spend a little more money by enclosing them in an envelope, the card will almost certainly get seen and read. How many people do you know who can resist unopened mail? Well, casting directors are people, too.

Composites are used mainly for printwork and they can help you get that kind of work if you mail them to ad agencies. You don't necessarily model clothes in this kind of work. Sometimes you just hold a product and smile. Sometimes you are a character doing something. A composite usually consists of three or four pictures of you in various outfits doing various things: a woman at work, a man with his kid or his dog, a woman of leisure, or a man with a product.

A composite is not a substitute for a headshot. It is a supplement to a headshot. Although composites are used primarily in getting you printwork, they sometimes can also be useful in getting you auditions for commercials. Rather than spending what will turn out to be a lot of money to hire a photographer to shoot the composite, I recommend getting together with some other actors with a couple of cameras and several roles of black and white film. Take lots of shots of yourself, perhaps over a few sessions, and then pick out four shots of you in action. Get 8x10s made of these shots and send them to the same photo shopwhere you got your headshot duplicated. A composite with four equal-sized photos on it can be cut into four postcards, turning five-hundred composites into two-thousand cards with four different poses for some variety. The shots can be of yourself exhibiting the kind of special skills listed on your resume, or imitations of print ads you see in the newspaper.

To get voice-over work you use audio cassettes pretty much the same way an actor uses headshots. You can have a tape made at a recording studio, and usually they can keep the mastertape for you and duplicate cassettes at a reasonable rate upon request. Call a few studios and compare prices for the recording session and for duplication costs. Pick the cheapest. The quality is not going to vary that much for your purposes. Before you record, practice at home, perhaps on your boom box. Find a bit of straight narration that you can read with a bit of color and texture in your voice, as well as a public service announcement. Then find a couple of magazine ads and read them as though you were doing them as a radio commercial. Your choice of material should depend on your vocal quality, and a good indication of what that vocal quality is will be found in the results of your market survey. After all, you talked to all those people who collectively determined your type. If they thought you were a doctor, find some doctor ads. You can go to your library and find magazines that appeal to doctors, businessmen, housewives etc. and photocopy the ads you want to practice with. (Don't tear the ads out of the magazines. That is inconsiderate of others and unnecessary bad karma.)

Eventually you will want to make a video demo-reel of your work on VHS. Don't waste money having one shot. It will cost too much and just look hokey. Instead, put one together from work you actually do. Each time you get a job, ask the director, as soon as you meet him, whom you should see about getting a copy of your film or video takes. The director will give you someone's name, mainly because he doesn't want to be bothered with such things. Once you have the name, tell that person that the director said to see him about getting a copy of your takes. Ask him what you can do to make things most convenient for everyone. Should you call the lab yourself and arrange to pay them directly? Do not take "no" for an answer about getting copies of your work. Bug them without being rude. These technicians won't want to be bothered with you, but they don't hire actors. If they are bugged that is too bad. It is your career and you will eventually need tape on yourself, especially in L.A. When you have some film and tape on yourself, have it transferred onto a 3/4" videotape, and then make copies on 1/2" VHS tapes. Five or six minutes worth should do it. Shop and compare prices from production studios before you do this. Give a couple of copies to your agent and carry one around with you to auditions. You just might have a chance to use it.

When getting started in the business, the promotional materials you will need in order of importance are 8x10 black and white headshots, resumes attached to the back, postcards with your picture, voice cassettes, and VHS cassettes. As soon as you get yours headshots you will need an office to work out of.

Setting Up A Place Of Business

What do you think of someone who does business out of the back seat of his car? Do you trust him? Think he'll stay in business?

You *need* an office to do any kind of business. Even novelists find that they work better when they go to a room which is reserved only for work. As an actor, the marketing part of your work, which is to say the great majority of your work, will be clearer and more efficient if you do it in a room reserved for business. Since you will not be receiving clients in your office but will be operating a mail-order business that takes orders over the phone, you don't need anything fancy. The room you use for an office should be as pleasant a place for you as possible, and you need a room where you can close the door. You also need your own desk, and your own phone with an answering machine or voice mail that you can check from a pay phone.

Your office can be your bedroom, provided you do not share it. Your mate's dirty socks sitting on top of your headshots will affect both your relationship and your career. It is possible for two people to share an office provided they both have their own desks and both treat the room as a place of business, but if you do that I would suggest that you partition the room. Good fences make good neighbors.

You can't share a telephone. Your partner will screw up your messages and this will ruin your relationship as well as have a bad effect on your career. Even if you have an answering service, you can not share a phone that is used for business. What happens when you both need to make several phone calls at the same time? You will pay more for the installation of your own phone, true, but think of it as a necessary set-up expense and be done with it. Local service after that is not so expensive that it needs dividing, and you will avoid hassles about who is responsible for what calls. In spite of what I have recommended about sharing a phone, you may have to be convinced the hard way. I did. You also need call-waiting. If you don't like getting interrupted, get over it. Call-waiting is now such a part of this business that anybody calling you for a job who gets a busy signal might actually think your phone is out of order and just call the next person on the list. The idea that if they really want you they'll keep trying is an affectation, the kind that kills careers.

You need your own desk where you can spread your paperwork around and come back later to find it in the same arrangement you left it in. You should not have to rearrange another person's droppings and vice versa. You just cannot share a desk, especially with your lover. You also need a readily accessible filing system. I recommend those hanging files in some sort of an arrangement where you can reach across your desk and get a file while you are talking on the phone. Important documents can be kept in a dust free box if you like. You will see the importance of files in the next section. I would also put a map of the city (or cities) where you work on the wall next to your desk, so that you can get directions on the phone and see exactly where and what the person is talking about. Also, looking at the map while you are thinking, instead of out the window where you are likely to daydream, will probably help keep you focused. Little pins stuck in the map at places where they do a lot of casting can help with this.

You should get a good stapler for attaching resumes to headshots, and a small paper cutter for trimming the resumes to fit. This is your job, not your agent's. A little porcelain wheel-in-a-well from a business supply store will save you eating a lot of envelope glue. Envelopes, large and small, as well as headshots and resumes will hang quite nicely in their own file folders. Your mailings should move across your desk like an assembly line production, even after you have popped a beer at the end of the day.

Your small business will also need a reliable delivery vehicle. Since the product being hauled around for lots of inspection and occasional sale is a human, the vehicle can be any one of a number of standard models.

In New York the public transportation system plus occasional taxies (and a good-natured attitude on your part) is sufficient. In most other places you need a car. Since almost no one who will be considering you for a job will ever see your car, it need not be pretty. The bottom line is that it gets you there on time. It needs to be safe enough to protect the cargo—that means seat belts—and reliable enough to start on a cold morning and keep going on the road to your place of work and then home again.

If you need an expensive car to feel good with yourself then you are perhaps an actor who will soon leave this business. I also definitely recommend getting a personal computer, as it will be extremely useful for filing, mailings, and updating your resume.

Your Other Job

"So, what do you do?"
"I'm and actor."
"Oh, really? What restaurant?

You should figure that it is going to take five years for your acting business to become established enough and profitable enough to support you without your needing an auxiliary income source.
Waiting tables, tending bar, and driving a cab are three of the most common other jobs that actors do. They all pay decently and you can do them at night, leaving your days free to make rounds and audition. There is a school of thought, however, which recommends getting a daytime job when you first go to New York or Los Angeles. The rationale is that you will have an easier time renting an apartment if they don't know that you are an actor, and since it will be months before you

get any auditions anyway, you will want to have your nights free to take workshops and do showcase theater productions. This will allow you to network with other actors and possibly to get seen by agents and casting directors. I agree with this thinking with respect to New York and L.A. and will make further suggestions about this in the chapters on working those markets.

Whatever other job you choose, it must be something which will pay your bills without killing your spirit, and which will eventually allow you some flexibility to audition. Week-end work is ideal for actors. I believe that you are well advised to pay as much attention to choosing and preparing for your other job as you do preparing for your acting business.

Here are some thoughts on possible other jobs besides the three mentioned above: Manage and maintain apartments. Real Estate sales. Any kind of outside sales. Temporary secretary. Photocopy stores with day and night shifts. Substitute teaching. Teaching anything you like to do, such as aerobics. Arts and crafts done at home.

There is another job which has a lot to be said for it and that is extra-work. In New York and other Northeastern cities actors have been doing it for years. Until recently, however, extra-work was considered a bad professional move for actors working in Los Angeles. It was thought that if you got known as an extra you would never work again as an actor. Now that SAG has jurisdiction over extras, that is changing, although if you do extra work in L.A. I would still advise you to stay away from the camera as much as possible. Just take the money, which won't be much, but which will carry other benefits with it. If you work two days a week as a union extra, you might make enough to get your medical and dental insurance paid for by the union. If you work one day a week as an extra, you might get credit for a vested year at the end of the year, ten of which get you a pension at age sixty five.

Most of an extra's day consists of sitting around (provided you have brought your own folding chair, otherwise it will be standing around). You can do a lot of your paperwork while you are waiting for that crowd scene to shoot. You might be able to send a postcard to every casting director in L.A. by doing three days of extra-work. However, don't write to them that you are busy doing extra-work. If you do extra-work, try to use the time productively instead of playing cards. Something you'll notice on the set: the ones who talk the most on an

L.A. set have actually worked the least. In the Northeast its somewhat different. A day's extra-work is often like old home week for stage actors in the area, and you can learn a lot there.

A final word on your other job: don't expect to get "discovered" working in the studio gift shop or any other place like it. You will need instead to get noticed while you are actually acting, and you will need to get noticed more than once before you really begin to have a career. Don't hope for a "big break." Work for a series of small ones.

V

The Actor As Small Business

For the moment I am going to assume that you do not live n either New York or Los Angeles. Perhaps you live in one of the regional markets which will be covered in later chapters.

If you want to do theatre in your neck of the woods, write to Jill Charles for her *Summer Theater Direcory* and/or her *Regional Theater Directory*. The addresses are in the bibliography. Perhaps there is a theater near you that will give you a job. Call them and find out their procedures for auditioning.

Perhaps you would also like to audition at one of the theater conferences that recruit performers, such as the Southeast Theater Conference. As I've said, I recommend doing theatre because the stage is where you learn to act and where you keep your tool sharp. I also think it is good for the soul.

If you want to make some money, however, begin by opening the yellow pages in your phone book and turning to the list of advertising agencies in your city or the city closest to you. (Wow, look at 'em all!) They hire people for print work, voice-overs, and sometimes for local commercials. Now flip to the video-production companies. (Damn, ten of them right here in town!) They hire actors for training films, voice-overs, and commercials.

Before you start calling these companies up, make a hundred copies of an *Account Profile Form* such as the one found below. You can either re-type it, or come up with a similar one of your own. Start thinking of potential buyers as accounts. The information you record on your account profile forms will grow steadily and will constitute your own personal goldmine of contacts and resources.

Account Profile

Name
Company
Receptionist   Telephone
Associates
Address
Best Route
Personal Descriptions
Personal Data

Shows Previously Cast

Currently Casting

Date   Transaction

Follow up

Date   Transaction

Follow up

Date   Transaction

Follow up

Date   Transaction

Follow up

Date   Transaction

Follow up

Don't think of ad agencies, production companies or casting directors, etc., as people who will discover you and validate your life. They are just doing business and so are you. Think of them as accounts which you are going to cultivate on a regular basis until they eventually buy something. Your attitude should be that you have a good product to deliver when they have a need for it, and you not only want to get the initial order but you also want them to re-order in the future.

You will not be able to make a living by working just one account. You will eventually need to open 100 accounts. Yup, 100. After three years of keeping in regular contact with each of them, say once a month with a postcard, you can start weeding out the less profitable accounts and concentrate all your energies on the profitable ones. This holds true for whatever market you decide to work and, incidentally, for whatever product you happen to be selling if you decide to change careers.

So there you are, starting locally. You have 100 "account profile" forms and the yellow pages open. Start with the ad agencies. Call them one at a time. When the receptionist answers the phone, begin making friends with her in your own way. Tell her your name, that you are an actor, and that you were wondering if her company hires actors and models for print work or local commercials. If they do, write the company's name in your file and tell her you'd like to send them a photo/resume. Ask her the name of the person who does the casting. Confirm the address listed in the yellow pages and get the zip code. Ask the best way to get to their agency and write that down. Ask what projects they have done that used actors, and what they might have coming up. Even if you can't get all this information on your first phone call, make sure you get the receptionist's name and thank her for her help. Then as soon as you're off the phone write her a "thank you" note - either a card, letter, or postcard with your face on it. Any salesman selling any product will testify to the importance of a friendly relationship with the receptionist. This is not kissing-up. This is standard professional courtesy.

What I am now going to recommend is controversial. Nevertheless, I believe that your first headshot should be delivered in person to the receptionist, if possible, after she has had time to receive your "thank you" note. This will give you a chance to smile and shake hands with the receptionist and personalize your relationship a bit more. Just drop off the photo and ask her to give it to the appropriate person she has told you about. Tell her you would like to come back for a general audition whenever it is convenient, smile again and get out of there. As soon as you get back to your car, take out the file on that account and write down what happened and what you should do to follow up. The least you should do by way of follow up is to send another card or headshot a month later and ask again for a general audition. Before any transaction with an account, look at your file on them to refresh your memory of past transactions, as well as the names of the people you will be dealing with and any personal information you might have learned about them. Did one of them just take part in an AIDS walk? Do they want to save the whales? Did you just see a project that they worked on? Again, this need not be kissing-up, but can instead be a genuine interest in them as human beings. Your attitude is what makes the difference. If you don't like them as human beings, the feeling will probaly be reciprocated. There won't be much reason for them to do business with you either.

When you have called the ad agencies, call the video production companies and do the same thing with each of them. Start a file on each one that hires actors. (Production companies that only shoot weddings usually don't hire actors.)

Once you have introduced yourself to the ad agencies and video production companies in your area, go to your library and get the phone books from other towns that you are willing to drive to for an audition. As a rule of thumb, you should be willing to drive two hours each way for a training film or a local commercial, and four hours each way to audition for a feature film, national commercial or TV show. The only way around these long trips is to live in New York or L.A. You will probably be able to arrange to car pool on the longer trips with other actors auditioning for the same productions. Other actors are an excellent source of information on who is buying what. Pick their brains even if it means having to pump their egos a bit. Consider this a friendly way of gathering information. And remember that God gave you two ears and one mouth.

Promoting Your Product

It is often said in this business that availability is even more important than ability. To get the job not only must you be available, but also the people who hire actors must know that you are available. When you are out of sight you are also out of mind. You will need to remind them of your availability. To do this you must stay in touch in a professional way without being a pest. I can't tell you how not to be a pest without knowing your quirks. I can give you some guidelines.

In selling yourself, a hard-sell will not work, but a persistent-sell eventually will. Even if you are sick in bed or suicidally despondent, you must spend a minimum of an hour and a half a day, five days a week, promoting your product by making a minimum of fifteen transactions every day with people who can give you a job. The transaction can be made in person, on the phone, or with postcards, but every transaction must be recorded in the appropriate client's file. Do you think that salesmen get by on their million dollar smiles? Wrong. The salesman who works the way I have just described outstrips Mr. Personality every time. Show this paragraph to any salesman and see if he or she doesn't agree.

Once you have brought/sent your headshots to scores and scores of people who might one day offer you a job, you need to stay in touch on a regular basis. You are a small business that not only produces a product but must sell it as welll. At this point you can not afford a sales manager. Do not depend on an agent to do the selling. An agency, remember, is a retail store where the customer is always right.

Let's look at the numbers. If you send out 15 postcards a day, five days a week, that's 75 postcards a week, or 300 a month—one for every casting director in Los Angeles or New York. If someone sent you a nice note once a month for a year, wouldn't you eventually be interested in meeting that person? So would many of those casting-humans. And just look at the numbers again. Seventy five postcards a week for a year, with two weeks off for vacation, equals 3,750 post-cards. Marketing through direct-mail usually yields a two percent sales return. That would be 75 jobs in a year's time. At union rates that would be $37K plus, not even counting residuals.

Do you know how many actors work this way? Almost none. Most pop a beer at the end of the day and bitch about the business. Ask yourself these questions: "Is my product not good enough to be competitive even with this kind of marketing effort?" "Do I truly want to succeed in this business enough to make this kind of disciplined effort?" "Will I be able to keep doing this for five years?" If you answered "no" to any of these questions some other vocation is probably for you, and you might as well know it now. Again, acting can be a delightful hobby; but, as you can clearly see now, it is going to be a damned tough business.

Your face cards are only one kind of promotion. Christmas cards are a must. Every business in America uses them and so should you. Other cards, such as Valentines day cards etc. are also appreciated. If you are in a play, enclose a flyer and a facecard with a note inviting the client to come. (If they are in the industry they will probably be allowed in free with their business cards.) If you get a good review, photocopy it and send it along with the flyer. If you have a TV episode coming up, mention it in your facecard, and if you ever see any of a client's work, such as commercial or film he or she has either cast or worked on in some way, send a card mentioning this.

Working in local commercials and training films doesn't pay much, but it will be easy for you to get copies of the film or tape of such work, and this can be put together onto a five minute demo reel which can be also be used for promotion. If you move to L.A. it will be tough to get an agent without such a reel. Since they are expensive to reproduce, these reels should be used selectively.

On the question of portfolios, I believe they are for models rather than actors. Many actors carry them around, but few casting directors look at them. Still, they don't hurt and they make a nice scrapbook of memorabilia that can serve as a reminder during the droughts that it is indeed possible to work.

No chapter on promotion would be complete without advice on interviewing and auditioning. There are numerous books out there on auditioning techniques, and since this is not a book on acting but rather on marketing, I will mention two books that I believe to be the best available: *Audition*, by Michael Shurtleff, and *The Perfect Monologue*, by Ginger Friedman.

Film and TV casting is usually done with cold readings rather than with monologues, but despite the fact that you will rarely be asked to deliver a monologue at an audition for a film or TV role, every actor should have five of them ready to pull out of the hat at a moment's notice. In order of commercial importance they are:

1. A one minute monologue that sells your type more than your skill. You can use this monologue for auditioning at big theater confer-

ences that limit you to one minute, as well as for those occasions when a film casting director agrees to see you at your request but has nothing for you to cold-read. The purpose of the one minute monologue is to create interest in yourself as a type and to get yourself called back to read for something else.

2. Two contrasting monologues of two or three minutes length which should sell your talent. These contrasting monologues should still reflect your type. They should contrast vertically rather than horizontally. There is absolutely no reason to contrast a sad plumber's monologue with a happy doctor's monologue if you will never get cast as a plumber. If you are a doctor-type, have an up doctor monologue and a down doctor monologue. This will sell your skill much more effectively.

3. At least one classical monologue in verse, again staying true to type. If can do something in verse that not only sounds like verse but also sounds natural you have a shot at doing some Shakespeare on stage. Even those who scoff at this are secretly impressed by it, and I believe that doing the classics constitutes the best training there is.

If you *really* want to do Shakespeare, have a second contrasting monologue which stays at least fairly true to type. There is no point in doing Romeo if you have recently retired. The two basic types in the classics are the nobility and the commoners. My advice is to pick one of those types and stay within it, at least until you have lots of experience.

If you are eager to do commercials, you might substitute a comic monologue done in a broad style for the second classical monologue.

When you are called in for an interview, you will be nervous for the first several times, but it will help to remember that this is only the first meeting and that you plan to be around for five years. If you screw up you will one day be able to make up for it. Think of the interview as a first meeting with someone you are delighted to meet, rather than as an interrogation in the judge's chambers. No single interview is a make or break situation, unless you display obviously rude or sloppy work habits. Interviews are beginnings. One thing you can do to help yourself relax when you are introduced to the casting director is to make a silent mental decision about how you would cast her if you were doing the casting. Keep this to yourself, however. You will feel and seem less self-conscious yourself, and will also seem like you are interested in the casting-director as a person. You will probably be asked to sit down across from her desk and she will glance at your headshot and resume.

89

Then she will say either "Tell me about yourself" or ask "So what have you been doing?" Answer in a way that is friendly, honest, and entirely positive. Do not make any negative remarks about anything if you can possibly help it. They are just not called-for in this situation.

Tell the casting director about the roles that you have played that you liked best, about your hobbies, and about aspects of yourself that suggest your type, but don't tell her what your type is because she feels that is her rice-bowl. Remember that affable is just as important as able. If she gives you something to cold read, ask if you can look it over for a minute and she will almost certainly say yes. Read your character's lines and make an immediate decision about what your character wants and is trying to do to get it. (Michael Shurtleff phrases this in an even stronger way: "What am I fighting for?") She will probably read the other character's lines in as neutral a way as possible so as not to interfere with your reading.

If you are called for an audition rather than an interview, pick up the "sides" as soon as they are available. If they are not available the day before, get to the audition a half-hour early and take the sides out to the parking lot. Make your decisions and then read your lines out loud so as to get used to the sound of your own voice saying them. It's odd, but your own voice can scare you sometimes. When you are called in to read, be friendly to everyone gathered around but don't offer to shake hands unless they offer first. Remember they are seeing lots of people. Again, the casting director will probably read the other character's lines neutrally, and again you will read yours based on what you have decided your character wants and is trying to do to get it. Remember that any decision is better than no decision. If you read well, they may have you read the lines in an entirely different way. It is a phenomenon that you will be able to change much more easily if you have made any kind of strong choice beforehand, whereas no choice, or nothing, tends to stay nothing. When you are done, smile at them all and thank them for seeing you, then walk out of there as if you'd been given the job. Go back to the receptionist and confirm the casting director's address so you can send a "thank you" note. It is even better to send a note to everyone who just saw you, including the receptionist. Record the whole transaction with as many names as possible in the appropriate file, including what you were wearing.

If you are called back, wear the same outfit. It worked the first time and they are not interested in seeing how great the rest of your wardrobe is. Your first outfit will actually help them remember why they called you back.

This is how you promote your product. If you ever get so hot that they are all coming to look for you, you can turn much of this work over to your agent, manager, and publicist. For the next five years, however, you are almost certainly going to have to do it all yourself.

Record Keeping

Omnes commerci en tres partes divisa est. I'm being a smart- alec here and paraphrasing Julius Caesar. He began his paean to his own accomplishments with the statement that "All of Gaul is divided into three parts." I have begun this chapter with the statement that all of business is divided into three parts. Those three parts are production, sales, and record keeping.

Actors love to produce their product. They don't like selling it very much because they don't like the accompanying rejection. As a rule they absolutely hate record keeping. So, probably, do you. Actors think that record keeping is greedy, penny-pinching, mercantile and boring. If you do what I suggest perhaps in five years you may be able to hire someone else to do your record keeping for you. You probably cannot afford that right now, and if you don't do it yourself—starting right now—your business will probably fail just as surely as if you waited around to be discovered rather than going out to sell yourself.

The best way to keep records is with a computer. Perhaps after a year of doing without one you will find the money to treat yourself and then deduct the cost of it from your taxes. To keep your records you need a minimum of three things:

First, you need a set of files on the people you will be doing business with, a separate file for each one as has been described in the last chapter. The very act of making a note in the client's file each time you have a transaction, even by postcard, will give you the lovely feeling of being on top of it all. Even during those periods when you can't seem to sell anything, you will feel like you are really a part of the business and knowledgeable about it.

The second item you need is a simple expandable file divided into the twelve months of the year so that you can keep receipts for everything that you might possibly be able to deduct from your taxes.

At the end of the day if you take five minutes to date the receipts and paper-clip them together with the others from that month, you can do your taxes in an hour at the end of the year as soon as you get your W-2s back. You might even have your refund in time to pay off your Christmas bills.

I am not a tax accountant and the tax laws may have changed by the time you read this book, so I would rather not make a list of things that you can deduct from your taxes. I would rather give you a few rules of thumb. The first is when in doubt, deduct it. If audited and the IRS disallows the deduction, you will have to pay the tax but they will seldom penalize you for a good-faith mistake. So what do you have to lose? I have a friend who is audited every year and who positively delights in the game. He smiles, and haggles and cajoles with the auditor, telling him jokes and having a fine time. Sometimes he has to pay a little more, and sometimes he wins every point.

The second rule of thumb is that if the expense helped you make money as an actor, it is deductible. The cost of workshops is obviously deductible. So are stamps, envelopes, stationary, headshots, photocopying, and demo-tapes. Parts of your phone bill and probably your answering machine. Mileage on your car spent looking for work, ie auditioning, making rounds etc. is deductible. (Commuting to a job is not.) The three-martini-lunch used to be deductible if you talked business, but this has changed. Check with your tax-man. Here is some good news—all movies and plays are deductible. Keep your ticket stubs.. Ask other actors what they are deducting. If the deduction sounds reasonable, deduct it yourself. Let's be realistic about something: you are probably not going to be making enough money in your first years to attract the attention of the IRS and probably won't be audited.

Your third absolute necessity for record keeping is a daily appointment book with a separate page for each day. The page should be big enough to write down where you went, who you talked to, and what you spent. This, together with saved receipts, will usually satisfy the IRS if you are audited.

You also need enough space on the page to list appointments. If you have a file on everyone, you can simply write down the person's name or the company name followed by (F), which tells you to look in the file to see what you have to do. It may be that it is time to send that person a postcard. If you have been business-like, you will have noted that in the file and written down the file-name in your datebook on the appropriately dated page. Over your second cup of coffee in the morning you have pulled the appropriate files and will be able to plan your day.

Yes, this kind of record keeping is a bit boring and requires some self-discipline. But if you feel you have a good product to sell on the market, do it whether it bores you or not. Tell yourself while you are doing this paperwork that you are making money by doing it. You just might not be paid for a while. That kind of thinking works for real estate agents and insurance salespeople. It will work for actors too.

Joining the Unions

The section on the unions tells you how to join. This short chapter will help you decide if and when you should join.

AFTRA advises you not to join until you have to join, and that means on the second AFTRA job that you do thirty or more days after the first one. You can work several AFTRA jobs within that first thirty days without having to join, but an AFTRA signatory is not allowed to hire you after thirty days from your first AFTRA job unless you join the union. In right-to-work states, though, you cannot be required to join any union.

Let me say again that once you join a union you are not allowed to do non-union work, even in a right-to-work State, despite what you may hear to the contrary from the misinformed. There is a list of union offices in the appendix and if you doubt this, call them up.

My advice is not to join any union until you have to join, but you should take the ethical question into account when decideing when you have to join. Will your conscience let you go on taking advantage of union benefits indefinitely in right-to-work States without joining? And don't you have to join to make that real commitment to professionalism once you have enough credits to do so? You pretty much have to join the unions to work in New York or Los Angeles, but my advice is not to go there until you have a decent resume of local credits, demo-tape on yourself, and then, finally, your union card, which you should get before you go to either of those cities. In other cities there is a fair amount of non-union work, and in some cities that is all there is. In such cities as Tallahassee or Columbia, SC, joining Equity or AFTRA can mean never working there again. What then? Are you going to go to New York or Los Angeles with a union card, a virtually blank resume and no demo-reel? Please don't do that. You will not be able to compete in those markets that way.

You may well decide not to join Equity at all unless your primary objective is to be a stage actor, or you get offered a great stage-role that you feel you just have to do. You do not have to join Equity to do Equity-waiver showcase productions in L.A. If you want to do stage work in New York or in the Regional Theatres you will have to join Equity to get decent roles. If this is what you want to do, I applaud you, my heart goes out to you, but I will not lend you any money.

If you get a SAG contract in New York or L.A. you can keep doing SAG work for a month without having to join, but after that a signitory is not supposed to hire you unless you join. After your first SAG job you can put "SAG Eligible" on your resume and seem virtually as professional in local markets as a member of SAG. You can also continue to do non-union work that way, build up your credits and your demo-reel, and then join SAG as you are about to leave for the big time.

An actor joining a union is like Caesar crossing the Rubicon. There should be no looking back. You should not join a union for egotistical reasons, even if you are made of money and the fees to join are not important. When you join you are making the statement that you are armed and ready to compete professionally with anyone. Join when you can honestly make that statement and are ready to prove it.

Listing With An Agent
I would suggest re-reading the chapter on agents at this point because your misconceptions about what to expect from an agent may have grown back. The chapters you have just read on finding buyers, promoting yourself, and keeping records may seem like too much work for a true artist and the little child in you may be saying "Mama, carry me!" Sorry, your mother doesn't work at the agency.

Once again, a talent agency is a retail store from which your product gets sold, but it is up to you to get the customers to go there and ask for you by name.

The first rule when listing with an agent is not to give an agent any money, not one cent, up front for anything—not for expenses they say they will have in promoting you, not for classes, not for photos or duplication, not for anything. Any agent who takes money up front cannot get a franchise from the actors unions. Such practices on the part of agents are considered unethical, and they are. Agencies who ask for money up front—and there are plenty of them—make their money by exploiting the naive dreams of would-be actors or their parents. They almost never get actors work.

Most small cities have modeling agencies which often call themselves "Model and Talent" agencies. Only a tiny part of their revenue comes from actually getting models or actors work. Almost all of their money comes from giving classes to models. They make their money primarily from the mothers of young girls who want their daughters to be popular and hope that classes in style, poise, and make-up tricks will accomplish that goal. Sometimes young career women also take such classes at night, hoping for the kinds of things that seem to grow in the human heart.

If there is no legitimate talent agency in your city you can list yourself with one or more of these model and talent agencies providing they don't ask you for money. Chances are there is a legitimate talent agency within a couple of hours drive from you unless you live out west, in which case you are used to driving longer distances anyway. Send these agencies a headshot and resume and tell them that you plan to hustle work for yourself but would like them to represent you when you do get work and would therefore like to list with them. This is good business for both of you. Having an agent, even in Podunk, makes you seem more professional and trustable to local video production companies and ad agencies. Again, most of them, like most of us, would rather shop in a store than buy things off the street. Having an agent will also insure that you get paid the going rate for your work, and, even more important, that you get paid at all. An agency can put the screws to non-payers better than you can.

If you get some work yourself and see that the agency gets a commission, you will impress the agency and make them think of you the next time that a job that you're right for comes along. These are the basic reasons to have an agent.

Since agents in different markets work differently, let's look at some regional markets and how the agents do business there.

REGIONAL MARKETS

Half the film production in the United States happens in California. The rest is divided among the other States. New York is second in terms of film starts. Los Angeles and New York divide most of the television production between them. Los Angeles shoots more series and New York more soaps. Series which are shot in other locations, such as *Northern Exposure,* which is shot in Seattle, and *In The Heat Of The Night*, which is shot in Atlanta, are done on location for both the local color of the settings and also for the regional accents of available local actors.

Florida and Texas each claim to be third in terms of film production, and each is slowly gaining on New York every year. The films shot there tend, with some exceptions, to be lower budget. Many of them are so low-budget that they are not tracked and counted among U.S. film starts.

North Carolina, with its Carolco Film Studio in Wilmington, also ranks third in the U.S. in terms of feature film starts, depending on which film-board you are talking to, and like Florida and Texas is a right-to-work State. South Carolina and Georgia are also right up there in the rankings.

Washington D.C. ranks third after New York and L.A. in the number of training films produced, mostly because of the number of them commissioned by the Federal Government. Washington and Baltimore together are considered one market and several feature films are shot there every year.

I want to reiterate my feelings about heading to the big leagues right out of drama school. Pick a local market first. I strongly advise against going either to New York or Los Angeles without your union cards, a demo-reel, and a solid resume. Each of those two cities is home to around fifty thousand union actors competing for available jobs, with another hundred thousand "wannabees" waiting in the wings. Why should they hire you there? Consider these regional markets first.

Florida

People have been wintering in Florida since the railroads were built in the last century, not only because of the wonderful winter weather, but also because of the beauty which the moist tropical air gives to the moonlight on the water and to the sun coming up in the morning.

Miami has also been around for a long time as a place for actors to work, mostly because of its cultural relationship with New York.

When New Yorkers began retiring to Miami they created an audience for theatre here, especially with the advent of dinner theatre. In time the resulting available pool of actors, both New York imports and home-grown talent, made Miami a good place for New York production companies to shoot commercials in the winter, and those companies and their offspring now shoot year round.

Miami has developed an infrastructure of actors and technicians which also makes for practical, efficient shooting of feature films, and many features are shot there. However, those used to operating on New York's "78 rpm" pace sometimes complain of a "vacation mentality" in Florida. An organization called the Professional Actors Association of Florida is steadily trying to correct that impression of Florida actors. They welcome new blood, and are a fine source for networking. Requirements for joining are membership in one of the professional actors unions and two professional gigs within the last year.

AFTRA and SAG both have offices in Miami. In fact, the membership of the Miami local of the Screen Actors Guild is now the third largest, after L.A. and New York. Since Florida is a right-to-work State, Miami is a good place to get your union cards. Producers can hire you even though you are not in the union, and that then makes you eligible to join the union. Miami, like New York and L.A., is one of the few cities where SAG and AFTRA do not share an office. Unfortunately, the lack of cooperation between these two locals hurts the membership of both unions, most of whom are actually members of both anyway. As a result there is no AFTRA/SAG talent directory, conservatory, nor available list of signatories, although AFTRA makes a signatory list available in its office and by the time this book is in print, it may have its own talent directory out. The lack of cooperation between these locals can only be described as infantile. With merger of SAG and AFTRA drawing nearer, perhaps one will eventually see this situation resolved.

There are about a dozen union-franchised agents in the Miami area and an equal number of casting directors. You'll find lists of them in the appendix. You will also want to subscribe to *The Florida Bluesheet,* in spite of its chatty and somewhat wordy writing style, in order to stay abreast of what's happening in the State. Many auditions of all kinds are listed in it.

Central Florida is the other main Florida market, but an actor trying to make a full-time living in Florida will probably have to work both South and Central Florida. The central Florida market consists of Orlando, Tampa and Sarasota. All the unions—including Equity—have offices in that area. Since it is only about an hour-and-a-half drive between Orlando and Tampa, actors living in central Florida can easily work in both these Central Florida cities, and there are a respectable number of commercials and training films shot in that area, as well as some features.

Universal Studios and an MGM/Disney partnership each built movie studios in Orlando as adjuncts to Orlando's theme parks, mostly to take advantage of the tremendous east-coast tourist traffic that goes through there. So, after visiting Epcot Center and Disneyworld, tourists can now thrill to seeing actual movies being made! Rather than make their own movies, these studios more often rent studio space to independent movie makers and TV producers, usually for productions on the low-budget side. Then, if a movie that is made there turns out to be pretty good, the distribution arm of the studio may agree to market and distribute it. If not, the studio still gets its rent and the tourist dollars.

Rumors persist that the entire film industry is going to relocate to Florida. These rumors first started after the Orlando studios were built. The rumors swelled again after the last L.A. earthquake, but such a move has not happened. Nor is it likely to happen, unless "the big one" drops California into the Pacific, and if such a catastrophe were to happen there is just no foreseeing what all the national consequences would be.

Florida, like many regional markets, keeps on getting a good share of film and television production since both industries seem to be decentralizing nationally. Florida is also attracting some European film production, and because of the bi-lingual nature of Miami, Spanish-language soap operas, called novellas, are shot there using Hispanic Miami actors. The novellas are then exported to South America, mostly to Argentina and Chile. (So why are you still freezing your butt in Chicago, amigo?)

Actors in both South and Central Florida often list with all the agents in their areas, and those willing to drive the four-and- a-half hours between the two markets can list with all the agents in both markets. As a result, the same actors are often submitted by more than one agent for a certain role. The actor will write down which agent she wants to represent her when she signs in at the casting office. It is considered professional courtesy for the actor to credit the agent who called her first for representation on the project, and to let the other agents know this before going to the audition.

Most agents in both South and Central Florida encourage actors to make rounds, to stop by to say hello and ask if there is anything happening for which they might be "just right." Casting directors in Florida, like casting directors everywhere, do not encourage personal visits, but some do hold general auditions during slow periods to take a look at actors who wish to be seen. Find out about which casting directors may be holding general auditions by making a few phone calls when you're in town.

At these general auditions, many casting directors want to see monologues since this is the fastest way to check out large groups of actors. Prepare a two-minute monologue that will make them remember you as a "type."

There isn't much action in North Florida yet. Despite the fact that the TV series *Pointman* was shot in Jacksonville, it is not geographically convenient for a full-time actor to live there.

There is plenty of theatre all over Florida, not just the nationally-known regional theatres like Asolo, in Sarasota, and Coconut Grove, in Miami; there are also dozens of small professional theatres, especially in South Florida, working under an Equity SPT contract or letter of agreement. Since Disney signed a contract with Equity, Orlando has become a potential place to get an Equity card; however, South Florida has a greater concentration of theatres.

The Theatre League of South Florida has a membership of more than sixty theatres of all kinds, Equity, university, and community, which are collectively known as "The Stages of the Sun." The Theatre League, a part of the Miami-Dade Cultural Affairs Council, publishes of list of these theatres and will be happy to send you a brochure. The phone numbers listed in the brochure are the box-office numbers. Call as many of these theatres as seem interesting to you. Have them send you their season brochures so you can see what shows they are planning to do. You just might want to audition. You can also get the number of the business office from the folks at the box office, and from there you can find out where and when auditions will be held.

Georgia and the Carolinas

For someone wishing to work full-time as an actor in this area, Georgia and the Carolinas should probably be considered one market. You will need a good-running car. The two most convenient cities in which to live are Atlanta and Charlotte. Atlanta has more local work, mostly voice-overs, commercials, and industrials. You can also fly almost anywhere in the world from its airport. Charlotte doesn't have as much of this kind of local work, but is more centrally located in the region and is closer to that big film studio in Wilmington, NC. In addition to your car, it will be a good idea to acquire some actor friends with whom you can car-pool no matter where you live in this market. This includes Atlanta, too, despite its subway system.

Atlanta, capital of the "New South," began to be important as a railroad hub even before the years of the Southern Confederacy. After the Civil War it remained a railroad hub and the main center of Southern commerce. After World War II, the city talked several airlines into doing as the railroads had done, and Atlanta kept abreast of the times. Georgia's highways, though, lagged behind the times, and some folks in the neighboring Southern States felt that this was a deliberate effort on the part of their neighbor to retard their own development. The federal government even came close to cutting off Georgia's highway money as a result.

Atlanta was the first southern city to reach a population of one million, and the city became the cultural capital of the New South. Film and video production companies sprang up there to make local commercials and training films, and whenever a feature was slated to shoot in the South, Atlanta was usually the site picked for the production office. Yankees and Californians were just as scared of the rural South as Southerners were of riding the New York subway, thus demonstrating that silliness is a human, rather than a regional, affliction.

The Chez Agency of Atlanta, founded by Shay Griffin, began as a modeling and talent agency and for years was the prime player in the southern talent agency scene. As the South developed, Chez continued as Atlanta's main talent agency and the main agency of the region. When the TV series *In The Heat Of The Night* came to town, they changed from talent agents into casting directors, and, I'm sure, still make a very good living.

Atlanta has enough happening for some of the actors there to earn their entire (modest) living through acting, just as the South and Central Florida markets do. Occasionally an actor might even become fairly well-to-do in any of these three places, but that is an even greater rarity than in New York or L.A. Atlanta has several equity theatres, though not a local office. SAG and AFTRA share an office there, and publish one of the dumbest newsletters you are ever likely to read.

There are several casting directors in Atlanta, Chez being the biggest, and several union franchised talent agencies. Actors list with all of them, just as they do in Florida. **"Betty Beautiful! Now available in all fine agencies in Atlanta."**

One more word about Atlanta's agencies. If you don't live in Atlanta they usually won't want to bother with you. That is not necessarily the case with Atlanta's casting directors.

The Carolinas

Despite the beauty of the beaches in this region, the inland city of Charlotte, after Atlanta, is the most professionally practical place to live.

Charlotte has a couple of small Equity theatres and more production companies and ad agencies than any city in the Carolinas. It is located smack dab in the center of these two States and is thus accessible to all locations in them. Several features, such as *The Last of the Mohicans* and *Dirty Dancing*, have been shot around Asheville, which is about two and a half hours away in some very pretty mountains.

Atlanta is a little over four hours away, about the same distance as from Miami to Orlando, and some Charlotte actors are willing to make the trip to audition. Car pools help.

Charlotte is about three and a half hours from Charleston, SC, where several features have been shot, from Civil War movies to *Prince of Tides*. Charleston is a lovely, historic city and many "movie people" are quite charmed by it, despite the cold shoulder they get from the old families of Charleston who don't like these movie interlopers, or their vulgar tee shirts.

Charlotte is four hours from the film studio built by Dino De Laurentiis in Wilmington, NC. There is an interesting story that goes with the studio and the two brothers that do the lion's share of the casting in the Carolinas.

De Laurentiis is one of the world's most famous independent producers. He was shooting for a while in Mexico and got tired of needing to pay bribes every step of the way to get anything done. This custom in Mexico is known as giving someone a "little bite" of the action, called a "mordida." De Laurentiis was looking for a location to shoot *Firestarter* when one of his lieutenants saw a picture of a southern mansion on the cover of *Southern Living* magazine . The lieutenant thought the mansion would look good for CIA headquarters in the movie and showed the picture to Dino. Dino liked it and they learned that the location was not only available, but available quite cheaply by movie standards. The mansion was located just outside of Wilmington, NC, a port-city which, at that time, still hadn't recovered economically from the pull-out of a railroad that was headquartered there.

Dino couldn't believe the prices, or so I am told. They had their location. Meanwhile, two brothers, Craig and Marc Fincannon, who had a friend at the North Carolina film board, got word that Dino was coming to North Carolina. They wrote to him and offered to do his extras casting. De Laurentiis met them, liked them, and gave them their first big production job.

Craig and Marc Fincannon, older and younger respectively, get along better than most brothers do. They worked summers together at an amusement park while they were going to college, and, since both of them were movie buffs, they bought a small movie theatre together. They began showing *The Rocky Horror Picture Show* 'round midnight', and made their theatre available to distributors at other times for screenings to be shown to local exhibiters. Then they went to work for Dino.

De Laurentiis was able to bring *Firestarter* in for something like

$3 million under budget, and he decided to stay put in Wilmington. He took the money, bought some land outside of Wilmington, and built some sound stages. Mark and Craig Fincannon opened an office downtown near the harbor, and have been the main players in the Carolinas ever since.

De Laurentiis's fortunes have always gone up and down, and the studio is now owned by his friends at Carolco, but Mark and Craig still do the casting. They receive submissions from agents from as far away as Virginia, Tennessee, and Georgia as well as from the Carolinas, and now they're getting them from Florida. They will look at a headshot or a demo-reel sent directly by an actor, but will accept submissions only through agents for roles they are casting. They don't want dual submissions, so pick one agent to represent you to the Fincannons. They will keep your headshot in that agent's talent book for referral by telephone.

If the movie they are casting will be shot in Wilmington, auditions are held there because the director will be there. If the movie is being shot elsewhere, the Fincannon's will usually hold auditions in a central location and the call-backs will be wherever the director wants them. Actors will usually drive great distances for call-backs. Working the Carolinas will mean a lot of driving, but food and rent are cheaper, and union scale is the same for work there.

Washington/Baltimore

Since the Federal Government can not sign a contract with the unions, the government training films made in this market are not strictly SAG films. The union approves of them anyway since the government agrees to all the provisions of a standard union contract. Union actors can therefore do them, and, since all provisions of a standard SAG contract are honored, the union will recognize such a contract for purposes of admitting a new actor into the union. This makes the Washington/Baltimore market a good place to get a SAG card and begin a career.

In my opinion, Washington is one of the most liveable cities in the United States. Unlike New York, where the subways look, smell, and feel like cockroach cocoons, Washington's subways are not only free of graffiti but actually have carpet on the floor. D.C. has monuments and museums, restaurants of every conceivable kind, concerts of music and dance that rival New York's, and the sight of well-known senators munching a hotdog. The summers are pretty muggy, especially in August, and a big snowfall in the winter knocks this essentially Southern city for a loop, but no place is perfect.

Baltimore is an anywhere, U.S.A., blue-collar type of town, known for its friendly bars and seafood restaurants. Most actors in the area live in D.C. and visit Baltimore.

Some Washington actors make do without a car, becuase of the city's excellent metro. Others feel they need some kind of car to reach Baltimore and northern Virginia. Rents in D.C. are higher than in Florida and much higher than in the Carolinas, but lower than New York and comparable to those in Los Angeles. There is a fair amount of theatre in D.C and Baltimore, both Equity and non-Equity. The more prestigious theaters like Arena Stage and The Shakespeare Theater of Washington (formerly the Folger) recruit mostly out of New York. In the opinion of Washington actors, this is due to the prejudices of the artistic directors of these two theatres.

There are usually about six feature films a year shot in D.C. and Baltimore, usually the exterior, or establishing, shots for stories that supposedly take place in the nation's capital. Nearby Balitmore can be used to shoot movies for just about any urban setting. As with many other feature films, the interior shots are done back in the studios of L.A. so the stars, cast, and crew can go home to their own beds at night.

This market is under New York's regional jurisdiction and in SAG films shot here the union dictates that half the extras must be SAG members. As I mentioned earlier, extra work done by D.C. actors on these films is like old-home-week, with lots of friendly chattering and catching up on the news. Washington also provides an excellent backdrop for commercials, and lots of them are shot there for that reason. New York companies also occasionally come to town looking for new faces, although the hope of getting "discovered" this way is not a good reason to move to Washington.

The big money for actors in D.C. comes from doing training films. The government, which includes the armed forces, makes scores of them every year, and so do many corporations based in Washington. Clean-cut types of all races, although mostly men with no facial hair, get most of this work.

If you like cities and feel that you would prefer New York to Los Angeles, it would really behoove you to consider going to Washington first, especially if you are the type described above. You can be a spear-carrier for minimum wage as an Equity membership candidate in D.C. theatres and get your Equity card that way in a year. You can also get your SAG card much easier in D.C. than in New York. Sometimes you can get cast in a government training film entirely through your own efforts and then be eligible to join SAG. You can live in a cosmopolitan atmosphere while you build up your resume, and because of its proximity to New York via an affordable train ride, you can make forays into New York before you move there. There is another advantage to D.C. which I should mention, and that is that it has the most helpful union local that I have ever come across. They really help actors there with such publications as lists of union signatories for actors, and a talent directory of actors for producers, and also with helpful advice on the Washington/Baltimore market. Once a month the SAG/AFTRA office has a special briefing session for actors new to the unions or new to the area. Nice, huh?

The Washington/Baltimore area has several franchised talent agencies, listed in the appendix, and it is customary for actors to list with them all. One last bit of advice: Dagmar, of Central Casting, might seem like a bitch-on-wheels when you first meet her. She's only testing you to see if you will come unglued. Continue to be polite and she will call you "darling" in a charming accent, and trust your professionalism enough to send you on auditions.

Join the Actor's Center as soon as you get to town for networking, classes, various discounts, comp tickets, a hotline, etc. Also, visit the Backstage Bookstore to shmooze, network, and, of course, to buy some of the books which I recommend in this one.

Chicago

Not many people go to Chicago to vacation. People go to Chicago to work, and work they do. In Chicago, even stage actors work. If you believe that theatre is an art which can give voice to the human soul, if you believe that theatre, like poetry, should engage the mind as well as the emotions, if you feel that you must work on the stage because your heart will continue to ache if you don't, then Chicago, rather than New York, just might be the place for you. Chicago supports more than a hundred-fifty theatre groups. There are other actors like you there, and they will understand you. Like them, you will be able to afford to pay the rent and you won't need to buy a car. You sure will need an overcoat, though, preferably a wind-proof one filled with goose-down.

Although Washington D.C. makes the third largest number of training films in the country, Chicago is third in the combined number of training films, commercials, and voice-overs made. That's the kind of work an actor can do in the daytime, leaving nights free for theatre. A higher percentage of actors in Chicago manage to earn their entire living from acting than in either New York or L.A., and that's something to think about if you just have to act, and especially if you just have to act on the stage.

Summer is the best time to move there, as it is anywhere. Hang out at Joel's Theatre Cafe, Sweet Home Chicago, the Scenes Coffee House Dramatist Bookstore, and Act 1 Bookstore. There will be audition notices on the bulletin boards, as well as offers to sublet and share apartments. You can list with all the talent agents, but get information on the agents first from other actors, and get *several* opinions on these agents and how to deal with them. Remember that *no one*, especially another actor, is the last word in this business. After you have an apartment and a phone, keep trying to make appointments to see the agents to show them your headshot/resume and a couple of well-tuned monologues. Meanwhile, start hustling, and keep hustling your own work even after you are listed with every agent in town or with one that you work with exclusively.

Seattle

When I called the Seattle local of AFTRA to get some information on this market, the lady jokingly said on the phone "Don't come here. You'll hate it. The weather is terrible! It rains all the time!" It rains a lot, to be sure, but more in terms of the length of its ten-month rainy season than in the number of inches of rainfall a year. However, the weather is apparently not bad enough to prevent an ongoing migration of people from relocating to this clean, pleasant, intellectual and cosmopolitan city. Locals have come to resent this influx, complaining that Seattle is being "Californicated," especially by people from L.A. The lady at AFTRA was good-naturedly voicing local sentiment. Local actors and technicians would prefer, of course, that film and TV production companies bring only their money to the area and hire everyone locally, but "it just don't work that way."

If you like herb tea, organic food, and intellectual conversation, and quietly assume a certain superiority over people who don't, then you will probably like Seattle. If you don't much care for these things and are not a political liberal, you may not be comfortable there unless you can co-exist with the peaceful, free, and groovy without talking politics. If it's any consolation, the city is also known as a place where you can get a really good cup of coffee.

Rents are not bad in Seattle, although crowding has pushed them up a bit, and the public transportation system is clean and efficient. However, most of these liberals still drive cars. There is a joke among actors in the area that they belong to the "I-5 Repertory " since many spend a lot of time on that interstate auditioning and working in Portland, Ashland, and even San Francisco, other cities where people are groovy just because they live there.

The Pacific Northwest is quite beautiful, and the rain is one of the reasons for that, since it's what keeps everything so green. I must confess that I like the whole area even though I have no particular politics. Somehow, seeing police on mountain bikes makes me feel all warm and homey.

Most of the paying work is AFTRA work, and the AFTRA office, by agreement, looks after the interests of SAG members. Actors list exclusively with one agent, so getting one is going to take some talking, first with other actors to do your research on the different agents, then with the agents themselves as they agree to see you. There is a good bit of location film work shot around Seattle, and TV series such as "Twin Peaks," and "Northern Exposure," now gone, and "The Commish," still going as of this writing.

There is also fine theatre here, as you have probably heard. The Seattle area has a dozen Equity theatres, and has the distinction of having produced the *The Kentucky Cycle*, the only play to win the Pulitzer prize before ever playing in New York.

Before moving to Seattle, write for a copy of *The Actor's Handbook: Seattle and the Pacific Northwest*, by Mark Jaroslaw. Read it to get the feel of the area, which includes Alaska and Montana, as well as Washington and Oregon, and then use the book as a resource directory once you're in the area. In Seattle there is a bookstore called *The Play's the Thing, Drama Bookstore*, which is a good place to check the bulletin board for auditions and room-mates. There is also a space there for staged readings, and a lounge to sit, read, and meet other actors. One hears the coffee's good there, just like the herb tea.

Dallas

Texas is another good place to get your union cards. The unions there are making a big recruiting effort to attract new members, unlike the locals in L.A. and New York, who sometimes seem to be trying to protect their current members by discouraging potential new ones. Also, the unions are willing to make concessions to corporations, production companies, ad agencies and theatres to entice them to sign union contracts. For example, companies are allowed to sign union contracts on a one-production basis, and Equity has an umbrella organization which makes it easier for non-equity theatres to hire Equity actors. The SAG/AFTRA office also publishes a talent directory.

Dallas has state-of-the-art production facilities which have attracted big-name film makers like Kevin Costner and Oliver Stone, as well as a good deal of television production. Hundreds of large corporations are located in the state, making for an excellent corporate, commercial, and voice-over market.

Texas is a friendly State with affordable housing and an optimistic pride in itself. There is a lot of tacky "new-money" there, which in Texas somehow doesn't seem offensive at all. Instead the "new money" just seems to be a part of good ole' Texas, like the cowboys who don't take their hats off in the restaurants. People from all over the country have moved to Texas and seem quite happy there, except perhaps for herb-tea-drinking vegetarians.

An actor working the Texas market will need a reliable car and probably a cellular phone because of the distances involved. Dallas is the most convenient place to live because there is more work in the combined Dallas/Fort Worth area than in Houston, San Antonio, or Austin, and also because Dallas is more centrally located to those other markets. An actor trying to work full-time as an actor will probably need to keep his or her hand in these other markets as well as in Dallas. With regard to the quality of life, Dallas is a million-plus city that is something like Atlanta in terms of climate and ambiance, but Texas is still, and will always be, Texas.

Before moving to Dallas, or to anywhere in Texas, write for a book called *The Biz Directory: An Actor's Guide*, by Mona Lee, an actress who lives in Austin. It will help you get the feel of the place and will continue to be a good resource once you get there. Also, if you move to Dallas, join S.T.A.G.E., the Society for Theatrical Artists' Guidance and Enhancement. (Yup) The reasonable membership dues get you the monthly newsletter and access to the hotline to keep abreast of what is going on in theatre, film and TV. You will also get a chance to showcase for casting directors once a month, and have access to other services to help you get started. They have a bulletin board, where you might find a room-mate, and a wonderful performing arts library, where you can do research and maybe begin a romance.

Fortress Hollywood

Let me begin this chapter by saying that everything you have ever heard about Los Angeles is true—all the good and all the bad, all at once. The greater Los Angeles area is a universe where you create your own world. You may have heard a New Yorker use the expression "my New York." If you stick it out in L.A. you may one day use the expression "my Los Angeles." Rather than being a New York world, which is narrow, cramped and intense, a Los Angeles world will usually be roomy, spread-out, and laid-back.

And superficial, yes. The biggest complaint about Los Angeles, besides the traffic and the smog, is the lack of intellectual life. L.A. is derided for being a phoney and superficial place, as New York is derided for being an aggressive, brutal place. Both descriptions are partially true and partially unfair. Rather than make judgements, my advice to you would be to bring a positive attitude to either place and then search out the things that make you happy.

Before going to L.A. I advise you to prepare for the move a year in advance. Going to either New York or Los Angeles "just to see," or "to try my luck" is like playing the lottery, which is easier and cheaper to play in your own hometown.

Before you go to Los Angeles, get your SAG card, a demo-reel of some of your work, and a decent resume. Try to buy the *L.A. Times* occasionally to check out the classifieds about rents and opportunities in terms of your "other job," as well as to begin getting the feel of the city. Then start saving your money for the move. You will need a car from the moment you arrive in Los Angeles, so you might as well bring one. Since as an actor you may be spending four hours a day in your car on a regular basis, your car should be safe and comfortable. Angelenos think of time spent in their cars as their private time. When you are ready to make the move, get your car in good running shape, and plan to stop in Phoenix to have it serviced by a AAA approved mechanic before driving that last leg through the desert. Many vultures who live along that stretch of highway claim to be mechanics and at first glance look exactly like human-beings. Pack your stuff in boxes before you head west and have them shipped to you via UPS once you have a place to live in L.A. With a good sense of humor, plan on shopping at thrift stores to furnish your domicile, perhaps in a "late student poverty" style of decor, rather than hauling stuff out there.

During that year of preparation, subscribe to *Drama-Logue* to begin getting the feel of the industry from an actor's point of view. Recommended reading is M.K. Lewis's book *Your Film Acting Career*. Read it before you go out there, and again as soon as you arrive. His book is considered one of the best around and you should get his viewpoint on things. Mr. Lewis likes L.A. and is a part of the Hollywood establishment. He also seems to be a nicer guy than I am, judging by his book.

The CD Directory is something else you should subscribe to before you go, and continue to subscribe to as long as you are in the business. The addresses of all three publications just mentioned are listed in the appendix. *The CD Directory* lists the names and addresses of all the casting directors in Los Angeles. It also lists all the TV shows being shot there, as well as who is currently doing the casting.

While you're getting ready to head out there, you might look up the TV shows you watch and look up the casting directors' addresses. Start sending them notes, not facecards at this point but perhaps postcards of your hometown. Tell them that you enjoyed the episode and that the casting was excellent if you thought so. Say nothing if you didn't.

Do the same when you go to the movies. The name of the casting director will be in the opening credits. Make a note of who did the casting and drop the casting director a note if you think something was well-cast. Why? Put yourself in the casting director's shoes. Wouldn't you be amused and pleased to get a card from Alabama or Maine complimenting you on your work? After getting a couple of those hometown postcards, wouldn't you be somewhat curious to meet the person who sent them if he arrived in L.A.?

Anywhere you decide to live in Los Angeles is going to be a kind of trade-off. For auditioning, the actual city of Hollywood is probably the most central and "convenient," in so far as anything is convenient in that traffic, but it is often called "Hollyweird." It seems to have more than its fair share of creeps. West Hollywood is nicer and more civilized, perhaps because it has a large gay population. Studio City is also fairly convenient and is full of all types of movie people. It is also hot and smoggy. Culver City is definitely worth checking out for economy, convenience and clean air. Santa Monica and the beaches have clean air, longer commuting times, and higher rents, except for the rent controlled apartments. It is said that rent-controlled apartments in Santa Monica are usually inhabited by people who were born there.

South and East L.A. are not viable choices as places to live because you need your car and your car will get stolen in those places. Beverly Hills, Bel-Air, Brentwood, Encino and Pacific Palisades are probably beyond your price range. Since you will presumably be a SAG member before heading out there, one thing you might do is write to SAG a month before you are planning to leave home and ask them to post a note on their bulletin board asking for a sublet or to share an apartment. You might get lucky. Don't send anyone any money in advance, though. You're not that lucky.

When you arrive, find a place to live, set up your desk and filing system etc., get your own phone put in, get a California driver's license and bank account (you'll need a credit card in addition to a California driver's license to open one,) get an "other job," get your headshot done and reproduced and your resume photocopied. Then go to Samuel French or Larry Edmund's bookstore to buy a copy of *The Agencies*, and *The Pacific Coast Studio Directory*. All this may take a couple of months to do, but when it is done you will have established your beachhead and will be ready to begin your reconnaissance operations.

Reconnaissance

Once you feel settled you can start networking into the industry. In this early stage in your Hollywood career remember once again that the creator gave you two ears and one mouth.

Joining the SAG Conservatory is definitely a good investment. It costs next to nothing. They'll tell you about the benefits. Start taking acting classes to sharpen your acting tool and take cold reading workshops with casting directors to start meeting them and also to watch other actors working. Start auditioning for Equity-waiver plays which rehearse and perform at night. Even if you do nothing but audition for

113

months without getting a part, it is still a good way to meet other actors. Joining the Actor's Center is another way to meet actors and to take classes.

You can buy *Drama-logue* at many convenience stores on Wednesday night, a day sooner than if you subscribe to it. I don't recommend subscribing once you are living in L.A. You don't save much money by subscribing and delivery through the mail is unreliable. Better to buy it at your local convenience store each week. Check the casting notices in *Drama-logue* and start sending out headshots. Job auditions listed in *Drama-logue* are usually not cast through agents. Sometimes agents put notices in *Drama-Logue* stating that they are accepting submissions for possible representation.

"What kind of agents?" is a question you should ask, though there is no single answer to the question of why a talent agency puts an ad in there. Sometimes an agency just happens to be short on a certain "type," perhaps your own. If the notice says "union talent only" and they are looking for your type, send them a headshot. If they are looking for non-union talent, you need to be careful. If you are non-union you don't belong in Los Angeles.

Remember going through the Yellow Pages, phoning all the local ad agencies and video production companies and starting files on the ones who hire actors? Good. You've had practice for what you will do with *The Pacific Coast Studio Directory*. Most of the area's production companies are listed.

Don't bother sending a headshot to Steven Spielberg. He will never see it. Don't bother sending headshots to those who the directory says make motion pictures or commercials. They cast through agents.

Call the ones who make educational films, industrials, or documentaries if you fancy yourself a narrator. Call them up, see if they keep headshots on file, make friends with the receptionist, who may also be the owner and the cameraman, and start a file on the ones who could one day give you a job.

Drop off headshots if you can, send them if you can't, ask if you can have an interview or an audition, and start keeping in touch on a monthly basis. Eventually you will get some action.

The people who make these kinds of films are usually friendly, honest, and down-to-earth kinda folks. They're nice folks to work with, and if you seem the same way to them they will, probably (eventually), be glad to hire you.

The Headshot Bombardment

There is a better way to get an agent than waiting for a notice in *Drama-Logue*, and that is to buy a copy of *The Agencies* at one of the bookstores mentioned and pick out the hundred or so agents that you think would most likely be interested in representing you. This little book describes most, if not all, the agencies in town, the kind of talent they represent, and what they specialize in, such as commercials or the representation of athletes.

Do not bother, at this point in your career, with submitting your headshot to the more famous agencies. Stick with the smaller ones, provided they are franchised. Write each agent a cover letter and mention the same kinds of things you would say in an interview with a casting director, such as the type of roles you think you are best suited for and that you are a disciplined, reliable actor. You can either hand address these envelopes or buy labels from the *CD Directory* if you have the money. Wait a week and follow up with a phone call asking for an interview.

Gird up your loins because you will be rejected by almost all of them. They will tell you that they have more talent than they can handle but to get back in touch in about six months. Nevertheless, probably before you reach # 100, one of them will take you on, at least for commercials. Its harder to get a theatrical agent, but one for commercials is all you need to start with.

Once you've got an agent, paste the agency sticker on your resume, over your own address and phone number, then make a hundred copies, and trim and staple them to your headshots. You are a now a professional actor, represented by an agent! Give twenty five headshot/resumes back to your agent and telephone at least every two weeks to see if you should drop off some more. That is always a legitimate reason to call your agent and it will remind her of your existence. Also, now that you have an agent, you can get your picture in the *Academy Players Directory*. This is useful in that your agent can tell a casting director on the phone that your picture is on a certain page and the casting director can look you up immediately.

You are now ready to begin your ground assault.

The Ground Assault

Get the latest edition of *The CD Directory* and make a file on each of the two hundred-plus casting directors listed in it. This is going to take hours and hours and hours, but afterwards updates will only take minutes. (And discipline) On the tab of the file write the name of the casting director and/or the name of the casting company for alphabetical placement in your filing system later. Then write the zip code of their address on the tab as well. The reason for this will be explained shortly.

I am now going to tell you to do something that is going to make these casting directors angry with me, but since I am not a part of the Hollywood establishment, I don't care. I am going to advise you to deliver a headshot personally to the office of each casting director and to put it in the hands of the receptionist, then to smile at her and get her name. If you try to deliver them in alphabetical order you will be driving back and forth all over town and will not finish this task until the second millennium ends. If you divide them into zip code order, however, you can plan your schedule so that you can deliver at least two and perhaps several headshots on each trip. Bring the files and write down the receptionist's name each time. That night, write a thank-you note to each receptionist you have met, thanking her for being so nice. Make a note in the file to send the receptionist another headshot in a week. Note the name of the casting company in your daily-schedule book under the appropriate date. When that day comes, get the file and send another headshot addressed personally to the receptionist. Write her a note asking if you can come in for a general audition.

Many, if not most, of these headshots will wind up in the trash, but a certain percentage of these receptionists will hand-carry your headshot to the casting director and ask if she wants to see you. Even if the answer is "no," the casting director will still have seen your name and face. You may not have made waves but you have made a ripple. Keep fishing and sooner or later you will get a bite. Ask any salesman.

At the rate of twelve deliveries a week it will take you months to deliver a headshot to each casting director. At the rate of one delivery a day, five days a week, it will take you close to a year to get to them all. Despite the fact that most casting directors say "no phone calls or personal deliveries," I think that you should do it anyway. What are

116

they going to do, yell at you?

All right, all right, if you don't have the fortitude to be that "pushy," then write a generic cover letter saying that you are new in town, are represented by such and such an agent, and that you would like to come in for a general audition at their convenience. You can buy casting director labels from *The CD Directory*, make them yourself once-and-for-all on your computer, or hand address the envelopes. You will get seen by fewer casting directors this way but will also suffer fewer face-to-face rejections.

Let me reiterate that casting directors are not going to come looking for you. They must know you are available for work. You have a product to sell, presumably a good one, and you have every right to make that known. Your product will be rejected ten times more than it is purchased, at least that much, but you must learn to smile and go on to the next one. Any salesman will tell you that you get a higher percentage of sales from phone calls than from mailings, and an even higher percentage of sales from personal visits. You will also get more hard knocks this way, and the best salve for such wounds is a sense of humor. If you are going to go for the higher percentages that a ground assault will give you, you must learn to take the punch and make a joke about it.

Nobody said this was going to be easy.

Showcasing and Networking

If you are acting in a play, invite as many casting directors and agents as possible. The whole cast can, and perhaps should, chip-in on mailing flyers and invitations to casting directors and agents. Don't expect many people to show up, however. The theatre probably looks like a rat hole. Nevertheless, doing such plays keeps your tool sharp and gets you networking with other actors.

When you get a job - a commercial, a training film, a small part on a TV show or in a feature - you have a bit of news to put on your facecards that you are sending out at the rate of fifteen a day (Remember?). When you are not working, send casting directors and independent production companies a thought for the day, or tell them all the same joke. Use your head enough so that what you write will be considered both personal and professional communication and not junkmail.

117

Your attitude should be that you are a part of this business, that you intend to stay a part of it, and that they should be professionally interested in such information. Use your own style to stay in touch, but stay in touch.

Showcasing and networking are about getting your product seen by potential buyers and then personally asking them to buy it.

Just do it.

VIII

Gotham

Let me begin this chapter on New York in the same way I began the chapter on Los Angeles: everything you have heard about New York is true, all the good and all the bad, all at once. Even more than in Los Angeles, you will have to create your own New York in many little ways, like walking home by a less direct route because it is safer, or perhaps because a certain block has a tree growing on it, and you like that tree. New York is a filthy, grimy city that seems at times to be dying of gangrene. It is also the most exciting place in the world. It probably has more in the plus column and more in the minus column than any place on earth. And it is not called "the city that never sleeps" for nothing. More happens in a day in New York than happens in most cities in a year.

Even if you are an adventurous type, however, who loves fast-paced excitement, I would not recommend going to New York alone. If you already have friends in New York, don't expect them to have much time for you once you move there. They won't, even if they had time for you on your last visit. And it is hard to make new friends in New York. Its reputation as a rude, brutal, cold-hearted city did not spring full-blown from a vacuum. Looking at the faces of the people on the streets and in the subways, one gets the impression that most New Yorkers spend most of their time tuning things out. People seem to be wearing blinders. Almost anywhere is a better place to be lonesome than New York. So go with a friend, or, even better, with two friends.

The rule of thumb with regard to apartments is that the closer you get to Manhattan, the smaller the space and the higher the rent. Manhattan, though, is where the action is, and time spent commuting to Manhattan in a crowded, filthy subway car to audition and work must be considered when choosing a place to live. When you start to see

what kind of money you will have to pay to rent the smallest and nasti-
est of apartments, you will go from feeling disbelief to being offended,
and finally to the grim-faced acceptance of the situation, coupled, one
hopes, with a resolve to make the dump as humanly habitable as possible. Two or three people can do that better than one. They can also
act as other eyes and ears for each other, socially and professionally. I
recommend going to New York together to find a place, and then going
back for your stuff when you have someplace to put it. Or furnish it in
"early actor poverty" style from the Goodwill stores.

A car in New York is nothing but a pain in the behind. The
insurance might cost more than the car. There will be no place to park
it. Alternate sides of the street get swept on alternate nights, and if you
forget and leave your car on the wrong side it will be towed and will
cost you a fortune to get it back. When you get it back it will be dam-
aged and will soon be further vandalized. Driving in New York is a
perpetual game of chicken and is not for the polite and patient. New
Yorkers stoically take the subway, the bus, and taxis when they can. They
also walk. In New York you must learn to keep walking without letting
others crowd you off the sidewalk. This will require firmness and resolve on your part rather than hostility, and is an excellent form of
assertiveness training for women. A book to read on the subway, sitting or standing, is a good idea for both mental stimulation and for
mental health.

The New York local of AEA has the largest number of Equity
members in the country, far more stage actors than there are jobs. Because New York actors are generally considered the best in the country,
many out-of-town companies come to New York to recruit actors. If
you are willing to live a good part of the year out of suitcases, then New
York is a fine place from which to audition for regional theatre work.

It is also the best place in the world to train as an actor because
of all the training available, but be careful of these workshops. Check
them out before writing the check. The *only* reason to go to New York
without a union card is to get this training. Then plan on going back
home to get your union card. Those few who get lucky enough to get
their union cards in New York may, with my blessing, stick their tongues
out at me.

If you have your union cards and are thinking about going to
New York, along with a couple of friends one hopes, get Mary Lyn

Henry & Lynne Rogers' book *How To Be A Working Actor*, which is New York oriented. Then re-read the chapters on "An Actor's Real Work" in Section I of this book, and Section VII on "Fortress Hollywood." Working the New York market will be much the same as working the L.A. market in terms of your marketing method. You will read *Backstage* instead of *Drama-Logue*. You will buy *The Ross Reports* at the New York Samuel French Bookstore and send out a mass mailing to agents in the same way you would in L.A.. Once you have an agent you will list in *Players Guide* instead of *The Academy Players Directory*. You will subscribe to the New York version of *The CD Directory*. And you will spend the same amount of time walking and riding the subway that L.A. actors spend in their cars in your attempt to deliver your headshots to the receptionists of casting directors.

You will work the New York market in the same way you would work the L.A. market, with a file on everyone who can give you a job, fifteen transactions a day, thank you notes, showcasing in small theatres when you can — the whole disciplined process. If you can stick it out in New York for six years using this marketing method while working a second job, taking classes, auditioning, and occasionally working as an actor, then your perseverance will probably eventually allow you to quit that second job, most of those classes, and some of the marketing as you audition and act more and more. Then you might have a twenty year career as a working New York actor, and that sure ain't chopped liver.

If you run into me somewhere, stop and say hi.

Break a leg, folks.

An Actor's Glossary
of Industry Terms

GLOSSARY OF INDUSTRY TERMS

Academy Players Directory: This is a Hollywood directory of actors. It shows actors' headshots and lists how to reach them, usually via an agent or manager specified by the actor. Actors must be union or be represented by a union agent to get listed, and the actor pays for the listing, which is inexpensive and worth it. A casting director can be told by telephone that an actor is on page xxx of the directory. There are four volumes to this directory, which is reprinted three times a year. The volumes list the following: leading women and ingenues, leading men and younger leading men, character men & character women, and kids. My advice is to list as both character and lead and pay a year in advance for all three "issues," but only after moving to L.A.

Action: The director's cue to the actors to begin the scene. They don't yell "lights, camera, action," anymore. These days it goes like this: The 1st Assistant Director yells "We are rolling." The camera operator repeats "rolling," and the film begins to roll. The clapper/loader claps the slate in front of the camera, which specifies which scene is being shot, and says "marking." The clap of the slate will be used to synchronize picture and sound later. The sound man will say "speed." The director will yell "background action," and the extras will begin to move. Then the director says "action," and the actors do their stuff.

A.D.: Short for Assistant Director. The A.D. is the 1st A.D., the one who co-ordinates the hundreds of details involved in a day's shooting, thus freeing the director to be creative. Some of the good ones might make as much as $10,000 a week. There is also a Sec ond Assistant Director, who is primarily an extras wrangler. On some days with big crowd scenes there may also be a "second second."

ADR: Additional Dialogue Replacement. A voice-over narration added to a film is an example of this.

ADTI: American Dinner Theatre Institute, the dinner theatre clearing house and central command office, located in Sarasota, Fl.

AEA: Actors' Equity Association, usually called "Equity," is the actors' union for stage actors and stage managers.

AFI: American Film Institute, a conservatory-type film school located in L.A. They have an agreement with the Screen Actor's Guild which lets them use volunteer SAG actors for free in their student films, in return for giving the actors copies of the film for use as a demo tape, a good deal for actors new to the area, who might actually be working for the next George Lucas.

AFL-CIO: The American Federation of Labor/Congress of Industrial Organizations, the umbrella labor organization of which SAG, AEA, and AFTRA are a part.

AFTRA: The American Federation of Television and Radio Artists. The union which represents actors and other artists who work on television and radio. This union also represents non-artists such as newsmen, who in this author's opinion belong in NABET, covered later.

Age Range: The range in the ages of

characters which an actor can play believably. The actor's real age is usually somewhere in this range, but not always.

AMPTP: The Alliance of Motion Picture and Television Producers, whom some think of as the capitalist bad guys in the black hats. Due to their efforts, film and TV are America's third largest export.

Art Director: The film equivalent of a stage technical director. He takes the Production Designer's concept and turns it into a plan.

ATA: Association of Talent Agents, a professional association created for establishing professional standards for talent agents, as well as for sharing information and promoting common self-interests.

Audition: Sometimes called an interview or a casting, an audition is a display of an actor's product to a potential buyer, usually a casting director.

"Avail": A non-binding term for an actor who is available (and usually eager) for a role.

Background: Human beings, also known as extras, who provide a kind of animated wallpaper as a setting for actors.

Backstage: The weekly New York show business journal which contains audition notices and other information of interest, mainly to New York actors, but also to others.

Back-up: An actor held in reserve as a possible replacement for another actor.

Beauty Shot: The final glamorous shot in a soap opera, over which credits are rolled, while neglected women start craving chocolate.

Best Boy: The one who keeps the time cards of the crew members, as well as a rolodex of possible replacements and supplementary help, sort of like a foreman's "trusty." There is a Best Boy Gaffer and a Best Boy Grip.

Billing: Giving written credit where credit is supposedly due, either above the title, in opening credits as the film or TV show begins, or as the ending credits roll, in that order of an actor's preference.

Bio: A short, narrative form of a resume, usually found in press releases or theatre programs. Actors usually write their own.

Blocking: The physical movements of an actor or actors from point to point in a scene. In film and TV these points are called "marks" and consist of two pieces of tape on the floor in the shape of a "T." An actor hits his marks when he stops at the "T."

Booking: A binding agreement between an actor and a producer for the actor to play a certain role.

Boom: The overhead microphone, usually held overhead on a long pole by a sound-man called the boom operator.

Breakaway: A prop or part of a set which gives the appearance of being solid but actually shatters or breaks off easily for effect.

Breakdown: Not an actor's personal problem, rather the detailed description of the roles being cast in a production.

Breakdown Services: An expensive, week-day publication, to which only legitimate agents and managers are allowed to subscribe. It gives the breakdown of roles being cast in upcoming productions.

Buyout: Payment in advance in lieu of residuals, usually for commercials.

Call-back: A second look, a follow-up audition or interview.

Call Sheet: A list of all required personnel and the times at which they are to report to the set. Issued daily by the production staff, usually with a copy for everyone listed on the sheet.

Call Time: The time at which an actor by contract must arrive on the set or designated location. Also, an appointment for an audition.

Casting Director: A purchasing agent, usually a woman, hired by the producer to go shopping for the best available deals on actors. See the chapter on casting directors.

Cattle Call: An open audition which usually turns into a mob scene of hopefuls. No one enjoys these things.

Changes: This usually refers to different outfits. If you are asked to bring three changes, do not show up with your lines re-written three ways. (As Michael Shurtleff once said in a workshop "Don't change the script. Their script is precious to them, every disastrous word of it."

Client: What the actor (supposedly) is to an agent. Also, what an actor (supposedly) is to the State worker interviewing the actor in the unemployment office.

Close-up (CU) The shot an actor comes to love the best, the one of just his or her face. Actually, the camera is your friend, so don't worry. They'll make you look good.

Cold Reading: The reading aloud of a script without much chance to prepare. "Cold" is how you feel inside under those circumstances. The more you read it, the warmer you get.

COLT: Chicago Off-Loop Theatre, Chicago's equivalent of New York's Off-Broadway, with similar contracts for Equity members.

Commission: The percentage of an actor's wages paid to the actor's agent or manager. A union agent may not make more than a 10% commission. There is no union regulation governing managers.

Composite: Several photos of an actor in different situations, used mostly for modeling and printwork, and sometimes for commercials.

Conflict: Something which causes an actor to be unavailable at a certain time. This can also be true after the fact. If an actor does a commercial for one product, this becomes a contractual conflict for doing a commercial for a competing product while the first product is still being aired.

Copy: The words to a commercial script, as in "This copy is idiotic!"

CORST: Council of Resident/Stock Theatres. The negotiating body for stock theatres that have a small resident company of actors. Some of these theatres are still alive and well, and Equity has a special contract for them.

COST: Council of Stock Theatres, like CORST but with no resident company. Both CORST and COST contracts are better deals for the producer than regular AEA contracts.

Cover Letter: What you should write when you send a headshot to someone, in order to personalize the transaction and thus reduce the chances of the headshot being circular filed.

Craft Services: The folks who fix the food on the set. Careful, it is possible to munch all day long and gain much weight.

Crane Shot: Using a crane to shoot the scene from overhead, sometimes with a sweeping motion to give a real "bird's eye view."

Crawl: The misnomer for how credits are shown at the end of a film or TV show. Credits actually scurry, rather than crawl, up the screen.

Credits: This term can refer either to the actually work an actor or technician has done in the past, or to the written acknowledgement on the screen of the work he or she did on a particular project.

Cue: For an actor, the signal to do your stuff.

Cutaway: A shot which "cuts away" from a scene to show something else and then returns.

Dailies: These used to be called "rushes," because they were unedited film footage which were rushed to the lab to see if the footage was good before moving on to other shots. Now they are called "dailies," perhaps to reduce stress. They are usually watched by the director and producer first thing in the morning before be-

ginning other shots to make sure they got what they needed the previous day.

Daily Variety: The L.A. trade publication which comes out week-days. More for industry executives than for actors, this paper reads something like an inter-office memo of the film and TV industries. They love cute headlines like "Webs Nix Pic's Tricks," as an example, which in English means that the TV networks have said "no" to something they consider offensive in a film and will not air it.

Day-Player: An actor hired for less than a week, the kind of work you will get at first. On your resume, "day player" will become "featured."

Daytime Drama: A kind of television program made with bored women in mind. The sponsors of these programs were often manufacturers of products which were once very meaningful for women, such as laundry detergent, and hence the name "soap operas." New York still has the edge on L.A. in the number of these which get made.

Dealer Commercial: A commercial made and paid for by a national company, then offered to local or regional dealers, who buy their own air time and air the commercial locally with their owns names inserted, or "tagged" on to the end, eg "Now available at Harry's Honda!"

Demo-Tape: Demonstration tape. Either an audio or a video tape made of portions of an actors work and used for promotional and audition purposes.

DGA: The Director's Guild of America, the union which represents Directors, Assistant Directors and Unit Production Managers.

Dialect: Misnomer for an accent. A dialect is actually a branch of a language which uses different words and expressions, but you'll still hear people in this business talking about a "southern dialect" instead of a southern accent.

Dialogue: Actually, a verbal interchange between at least two characters, but used in show business to refer to any words spoken by an actor.

Director: In film and TV, the person whose primary job is to tell the story in pictures. The Director, not the Director of Photography, chooses the camera angle, lens, and composition of the shot. In theatre, film, and TV, the Director is also the person who coordinates all artistic elements into one artistic vision, or at least is supposed to do that.

Dolly: A kind of cart, pushed by a person called a dolly grip, which carries the camera smoothly forward or backward on a track. A dolly shot brings the spectator to what is being filmed, while a zoom seems to bring the subject to the spectator.

Donut: A change which is inserted into a commercial rather than at the end of it.

Double: A performer who resembles another performer and is used in his or her place, as in "stunt-double."

Downgrade: The reduction of an actor to an extra. This is not allowed by the union. Verbal downgrading behind another's back is a constant part of show business, however.

D.P.: The Director of Photography, also called the cinematographer. The D.P.'s job is to light the set. Gaffers and grips, covered later, report to him.

Drama-Logue: L.A.'s equivalent of *Backstage*. A weekly newspaper containing casting notices, reviews, and articles about the industry. A must for the L.A. actor.

Dressing the Set: Adding furniture, props, and whatever else is necessary to make the set look realistic.

Drive-on-pass: Written permission to drive a vehicle onto a studio lot or film set.

Drop/pickup: A type of contract which allows a film production to hire an actor, lay him off, and then rehire him again on the same film. This doesn't happen very much. Usually actors are paid for those in-between-days even though they are not actually working.

Dupe: A duplicate of a film or tape, not a misused person.

Eight by Ten (8x10): A photograph 8x10 inches used for audition purposes.

Eighteen to play younger: The description of an actor who is at least eighteen years old, and thus is not subject to child labor laws, but who looks younger and can convincingly play a younger character.

Electrician: The electrician on a film is called the gaffer. Electricians hang and focus lights and plug things in.

Emancipated Minor: A kid who has been given permission by the courts to make his or her own decisions, and for the most part has the legal status of an adult.

129

Employer of Record (EOR): Professional accounting organizations responsible for issuing checks and W2s to actors.

Equity: The term by which Actors' Equity Association is usually referred.

Equity Waiver: As in "Equity Waiver Contract" or "Equity Waiver Theatre." These are small L.A. theatres seating 99 or less which do not have to comply with most provisions of regular equity contracts. Actors usually work in these theatres trying to showcase themselves for film work, as discussed in the section on Fortress Hollywood.

Exclusivity: Sole rights granted by an actor to an agent, or by an actor to a commercial producer with regard to not making commercials for competitive products.

Executive Producer: The person who puts the financial deal together to get a film or TV program made.

Exhibit A: The part of the AFTRA Network Code which covers prime time TV, AFTRA's equivalent of SAG's Basic Television Agreement for TV shows shot on film.

EXT.: Exterior. A scene which is to be shot outside.

Extras: Human beings who are treated like cattle. Experienced extras keep their sense of humor, bring lawn chairs and a deck of cards, something to read, or some paperwork to do.

Field Rep: Someone from the AFTRA or SAG office who visits the set to insure that producers are complying with their contracts.

First Refusal: A non-binding courtesy extended to a producer with regard to an actor's availability. The actor gives the producer "first refusal" before accepting another job.

Five out of seven: A five day work week which does not necessarily begin on Monday.

Fixed Cycle: A thirteen week period for which a commercial producer pays an actor for the use of his image on tape or film.

Flipper: False teeth for kids with baby teeth. Also a porpoise rumored to be making a comeback.

Forced Call: A requirement to return to the set less than 15 hours after being dismissed. This results in an actor getting an extra whole day's pay!

Foreign Replay: Re-runs outside the U.S. and Canada for which actors are paid residuals.

Four "A"s: Associated Actors and Artists of America. A mini-umbrella organization inside the AFL/CIO comprised of the performers' unions.

Franchised Agent: An agent that AEA, AFTRA, or SAG approves of as a certified good person. The union does a background check for a criminal record and a credit check on agents wishing to be franchised so they can represent union talent.

Free-lancing: Working without either a full-time employer or an exclusive agent, i.e. the way most actors work.

FX: The script or contract notation for effects, i.e. special effects.

Gaffer: The gaffer is the chief electrician on a film crew who reports directly to the Director of Photography. A gaffer is one of his crew members.

General Interview: An audition for a casting director, but with no specific project in mind. An actor requests this in the hope that he or she will be remembered by the casting director at a later time when something comes along for which the actor is "right." Casting directors may grant general interviews when they are not busy with other things.

Glossy: An 8x10 headshot with a shiny finish.

Gofer: Someone, usually attached to the production office, who runs errands, goes fer this, goes fer that.

Golden Time: This is overtime after the 16th hour on the set.

Grip: A cross between a construction worker and a moving man. A grip is a crew member who moves pieces of the set around, and either moves or builds things for the electricians to hang lights on. It should be noted that not all grips are Neanderthals.

Guaranteed Billing: The type and position of credit given an actor for a performance, usually negotiated into an actor's contract by an agent. eg An opening credit with "Guest Star" billing.

Hand Model: Someone with photogenic hands for commercials. There is money in this, and also for hair, teeth, and occasionally feet.

HAT/BAT Contract: Hollywood Area Theatre/Bay Area Theatre Contracts, similar to COLT and Off-Broadway contracts.

Hollywood Reporter: *Daily Variety's* competitor, as *Newsweek* is to *Time.*

Head Shot: An 8x10, black and white, head and shoulders photo of an actor, without which he or she is not a professional.

Hiatus: The period in which a TV show is not in production. (To say that an actor is in hiatus is usually an unnecessary redundancy; it is one of the basic assumptions of the industry.)

Hold: A binding, contractual stipulation that an actor be available for a job.

Holding Fee: What an actor is paid for the above.

Honey Wagon: A towed vehicle where you find the toilets.

IATSE: International Alliance of Theatrical Stage Employees. Called IA on the west coast, and Yatsee on the east, this is the union to which most crew members belong, such as camera crew, gaffers, grips, makeup artists, etc. Drivers belong to the Teamsters.

Industrial: A non-broadcast film or tape used primarily for educational or training purposes. Also called training films and corporates.

Inserts: A shot which will be inserted into other footage, perhaps of hands doing something, or of an object important to the story. Directors will sometimes shoot an insert first thing in the morning so that when studio execs come to work they will hear that a production has already gotten its first shot of the day. The director hopes that the execs will therefore not come down to the set to hassle him.

INT.: Interior. Script notation for an indoor location. Every scene in a screenplay is noted DAY or NIGHT, INT. or EXT.

In-Time: The time an actor or crew member is due, or due back, on the set. Same as call-time.

Lift: Using, or "lifting" footage from one project to another. Often done with commercials.

Liquidated Damages: What producers owe to actors, et al, when they don't fulfill their contractual obligations. Unions usually require a bond to make sure actors get paid this money.

LORT: League of Resident Theatres. These are non-profit theatres of various sizes located throughout the country which, in league with one another, negotiate collectively with Equity.

Long Shot: (LS) This doesn't refer to an actors chance for success, but rather to a camera angle which shows the actors whole body, as opposed, say, to a close-up, or a "two-shot" which shows two actors from about the waist up. This last shot, by the way, is called "an American shot" in France.

Looping: Matching sound to picture in a post production studio.

Manager: With respect to actors, this person is something between a sales representative and a therapist. This person may not negotiate a contract for an actor. An agent or a lawyer must do that. Since managers are not regulated by the unions, he or she may charge more than a 10% commission on an actor's earnings. Nevertheless, many actors, especially stars, have managers.

Matching: This terms refers to the casting of actors whose physicality matches, in casting a family, for instance.

Meal Penalty: A monetary bonus paid by the producer to union actors or union extras for not feeding them within six hours of their call-time.

Monologue: In show biz, any speech by a single actor. Playwrights write monologues for exposition purposes. Actors use them for audition purposes. Hint: Think of a monologue as an outburst, and know what caused it.

MOS: "Mit out sound," as imported German directors used to say back in the thirties. Also stands for "motion only shot," which amounts to the same thing.

M.O.W.: Movie of the Week. A two-hour, made for TV movie comprised of six acts and five cliff-hangers which get followed by commercials. The themes are usually about some topical issue, a crime of the week, a disease of the week, etc.

NABET: National Association of Broadcast Employees and Technicians, the union to which all broadcasters should belong instead of AFTRA so as not to impede AFTRA's merger with SAG.

National Commercial: A commercial which will be aired nationwide, meaning big-bucks for the actor. Commercials which will be aired in New York or L.A. are automatically considered national commercials.

Network Approval: A rare instance in which the network reserves the right to consent to the actor being cast in a certain role.

132

Non-Equity: Actors which are not members of AEA, or theatre productions which have not signed agreements with AEA. Equity actors may not work in such productions.

Network Code: AFTRA's contract with the networks. Among TV execs, this term might refer to their own professional standards, but actors are more concerned with the first definition.

Night Premium: A 10% bonus paid to union actors for work performed (or for being on the clock) after 8 PM.

Nomex: Fire-proof long-underwear used by stuntmen.

Off-Broadway: New York theatres of less than 500 seats located outside the theatre district.

Off-Off-Broadway: An eclectic bunch of small, threadbare, often experimental New York theatres found throughout the city. Many hang on by operating under Equity's "Showcase Code," where actors work for free in order to get seen. If you go to New York to work as an actor, you will become very familiar with these theatres.

Off-Camera (OC or OS for "Off-Stage"): Dialogue or sounds heard but not seen.

Open Call: Auditions open to all actors whether or not they have been submitted by agents.

Out Clause: A contractual clause which lets someone get out of a deal.

Out of Frame: A location which is not in view of the camera.

Out-Time: The official time when an actor is no longer on the clock. This is after an actor has changed out of wardrobe and reports back to the 2nd AD, not when the 2nd AD first says "You're wrapped." Check this out-time on the sheet as you sign out.

Overdubbing: Putting a new soundtrack over an existing one, like in a record studio for a commercial.

Overtime (OT): Usually any time on the clock over eight hours a day or forty hours a week.

P.A.: Production Assistant. These people are gofers with walkie talkies and fanny packs who take orders from Assistant Directors. Sometimes they actually know what they are doing.

Pages: Parts of a script, often rewritten, containing specific scenes.

Pan: A sweeping motion of the camera, like turning your head.

P&G: Proctor & Gamble. This refers to a squeaky clean, all-American, white bread WASP look in an actor.

Pay or Play: A clause in a contract which stipulates that you get paid even if you don't work.

Paymaster: A union-approved employer of record. Sometimes a non-union company wishing to hire a specific union actor will hire him or her through a paymaster and abide by union rules for this one actor.

Pension and Health: An additional 12% of an actor's salary a producer is required to pay towards an actor's health insurance and retirement fund.

Per Diem: Money paid by the day to actors for meals not provided by the producer, usually for breakfast and supper.

Photo-Double: An actor hired for various reasons to perform in the place of another actor because he or she looks like that actor.

Pick Up: A shot that is needed to catch up with the production schedule, usually a shot that needs to be redone.

Picked Up: Signed up. Given a contract. This applies to actors for a production, and also to TV series which get slated or re-newed for a season.

Pilot: In TV jargon, the first show of a potential series which introduces the characters and the show's setting.

Players Guide: The New York equivalent of *The Academy Players Directory*.

Plosive(s): The letters p,b,t,d,k,g, all of which make a popping sound when pronounced. Some actors doing voice-over work turn slightly away from the microphone when speaking these letters in order to minimize this sound.

POV Shot: Point of view shot, sometimes called an over-the-shoulder shot because that is where the camera is placed. It tells the audience what a character is seeing.

Prime Time: The hours when most people watch TV, 8-11 pm EST, 7-10 CST.

Principal: An actor who either speaks, or performs special business to advance the story.

Producer: The person at whose desk "the buck stops." That's why this person picks up the award for "Best Picture." This person's desk is also the place where the buck starts. He or she hires everyone in the production.

Product Conflict: A situation which an actor is contractually obligated to avoid in commercials, that of promoting two competitive products.

Production Contract: Standard Equity contract for a single Equity production. A producer must pay higher minimums under this kind of contract, and it is thus in the producer's interest to try to get another kind of contract, such as a LORT or CORST contract.

Production Designer: Sometimes called "an Art Director who knows the producer," this person comes up with the concept, the vision of what the setting should look like. His drawings look like art work, whereas the Art Director's drawings look like blueprints.

Props: Properties. Objects placed on a set for use in the story which are not part of the set decor. If the object is touched or referred to it is a prop and not a set piece.

Prop Master: The person who finds props and keeps track of them. If you abuse a prop, this person will abuse you.

PSA: Public Service Announcement. Note that SAG and AFTRA actors are not permitted to do these "simply as a public service" without also being paid to do them.

Quote: The money an agent asks for an actor's services. Also, any price anyone quotes for anything.

Ratings: The number of people watching or listening to a certain program at a certain time.

Regional Commercial: A commercial which will be aired only in a certain area of the U.S. (There would be no point in airing a snowmobile commercial in Florida, for instance.) These commercials cost less to make and to air, and consequently actors are paid less to do them, but actors still get paid more for these than for a local commercial.

Release: The end of a contractual obligation. This term can refer to the end of a day's work, to a commercial being taken off the air and thus allowing the actor to do a commercial for a competitor, or to other provisions of a contract.

Release Letter: Most often, this refers to a letter sent by an actor to an agent telling the agent good-bye.

Rerun: The rebroadcast of a TV program.

Residual: Additional money paid to an actor when a commercial, TV show, or film is shown again, or a radio spot airs again.

Resume: Professional information which an actor attaches to the back of an 8x10 headshot, including credits, training, etc. See the chapter on resumes.

Reuse: Rebroadcast of a commercial.

Rewrite: Changes in the script. In a film script, these changes use color coded paper and by the end of the shoot the script looks like a rainbow.

Right-to-Work States: States which do not permit closed-shop contracts. See the chapter on unions.

Running Part: A recurring role in a TV series.

Rounds: As in "making rounds." Going from place to place, dropping off headshots while bravely trying to smile.

SAG: The Screen Actors Guild.

Scale: The minimum a union actor can be paid for a job. This includes the producer's 12% contribution to the actors pension and welfare fund.

Scale plus10(%): The actual amount it costs the producer to hire a union actor. Since to take the 10% agent's commission out of the actor's pay would mean that the actor would make less than the minimum allowed, the producer must actually pay scale plus 10. This does not apply to commercials or industrials.

Screen Test: These days, a videotape made to see how an actor would look in a certain role.

Script: The written form of a story which will be performed on stage, screen, television or radio.

Script Supervisor: The secretary on the set, although they won't like this description. She makes a record of everything that happens on the shoot with regard to shooting the script, including such things as the type of lens used for each take, any changes in dialogue, etc, etc.

Session Fee: Initial money paid to an actor for performing in a commercial. Residuals come later.

Set: Where the action is. This can be a specially constructed indoor scene, but the term also refers to an outdoor location where something is being filmed or taped. In the middle of a field, the AD will still say "Quiet on the set," before the camera rolls.

Set decorator: The person directly under the Art Director who finds the necessary materials to build and decorate the set, and who supervises the swing gang in building it.

Set Teacher: Sometimes called a studio teacher. A tutor hired to teach kids on the set. Also responsible for enforcing child labor laws. Not all States require set teachers.

SFX: Notation for sound effects, not special effects, which is FX.

Showcase: A theatre performance where actors work for free hoping to get seen.

Sides: Parts of a script, used mostly for auditions and day-players.

Sight and Sound: The right of the parent of a child performer to remain within sight and sound of the child, i.e. to be on the set whether you like it or not.

Sign-in Sheet: A written record of who has auditioned. Actors auditioning for AFTRA and SAG jobs should remember to sign out as well, in that they may be entitled to compensation if kept more than an hour at the audition.

Signatory: A producer who signs a union contract.

Silent Bit: Action performed by an extra which advances the story, such as a waiter serving something to a character. This gives the extra a little more money, called a "bump." In a commercial, the performer might be paid as a principal for performing the same action.

Single Card: A special credit in a film or TV show in which only one actor's name appears.

Sit Com: Situation Comedy. See the chapter on television.

Slate: A little chalkboard with a black and white striped clapper used to identify film or TV takes. Also, a verb, as in "slate yourself." This means the camera is rolling and you should say your name and give the name of your agent if that is appropriate.

Soap(s): See Daytime Dramas.

Soundtrack: In film or TV, the separately recorded audio portion.
To call an audio tape for radio a soundtrack would be a redundancy.

Special Business: A specific action by an extra or actor which advances the story. See Silent Bit.

Spot: A commercial.

SSDC: Society of Stage Directors and Choreographers. A professional association which sets standards for, and promotes the common interests of, stage directors and choreographers. This organization is a professional association but not a union.

Stage Right and Stage Left: Looking at the audience, stage right is to your right, stage left is to your left, down stage is in front of you, and up stage is behind you.

Stage Manager: In theatre, the person who takes over from the director and runs the show after it opens. In film or TV, the stage manager is a custodian/facilities manager. It is a hard, thankless job on stage or in the studio, and one deserving of admiration and respect.

136

Station 12: The part of the Screen Actors Guild which assures that actors are paid up members and clears them to work on SAG productions.

Station 15: The part of the Screen Actors Guild which assures that prospective employers of SAG talent are signatories.

Standard Union Contract: A contract, previously negotiated between the unions and the producers, which stipulates minimum acceptable pay and working conditions for union actors.

Standards and Practices Department: The network censors.

Stand-In: In some countries this person is called a lighting double. A stand-in is special extra, about the same size and coloring as a principle actor, who stands on an actor's marks and walks through the actors blocking while the lights are being set. This is a great job for someone just starting out. Since you are there to watch the shot rehearsed and set up, it is like being paid to go to film school. Work well with the crew and the director will probably give you a line in the movie, thus making you eligible for your union card.

Storyboard: A script in comic book form.

Studio: A room, a sound stage, a whole building, or a group of buildings used for recording, taping or filming. The plural, "the studios," refers to the seven major Hollywood film studios.

Stunt Coordinator: The person charged with the design, coordination, and supervision of stunts and other dangerous activities. These guys are usually independent contractors with their own teams of stuntfolks.

Stunt-Double: A stuntman or woman who resembles a principal actor and performs a dangerous activity in that actor's place.

Submission: Offering or suggesting an actor for a role, usually done by an agent to a casting director.

Syndication: The practice of selling TV shows to individual TV stations or cable companies rather than to the networks.

Taft-Hartly: As in "We can Taft-Hartly you." The practice of allowing non-union actors to work on a union project as stipulated by certain provisions of the Taft-Hartly Act.

Tag: An announcement which is "tagged" to, or added to, the beginning or end of a commercial or TV show, as in "Now available at XYZ Superstore, right here in town!"

Take: A shot, as in "take a picture." A "take" is the filming of, or video-taping of, an action sequence. The sequence may have to be re-shot many times, ie will require many takes, before they get what they want.

TCG: Theatre Communications Group. An organization funded by the Ford Foundation which acts as an audition clearing-house for regional theatres who have come to New York to recruit actors. They hold general auditions a couple of times a year, and then have call-backs for specific castings.

TYA: Theatre for Young Audiences. An equity contract for producers of children's theatre.

137

Teleprompter: Actually a brand name. A piece of equipment which scrolls text upward, allowing the narrator to read it while looking at the camera.

Test Market: There are many business connotations for this term, but for an actor's purposes let us say that this term refers to airing a commercial in only one market to test its effectiveness. If successful, the commercial may then be aired in other markets, resulting in more money for the actor.

Tight Shot: A close up of something, either an actors face or an object, etc. "Go in tight on his hand."

Theatrical: TV or film work, rather than corporate or commercial work. Some actors have a theatrical agent and a commercial agent.

Three Quarter (3/4") tape: Video tape for professional use. Something may be shot on 3/4" tape and then duplicated onto 1/2" tape for viewing on regular VCRs.

Trades: Publications geared for people who work in the entertainment industry.

Turnaround: For an actor, this term refers to the time between actual dismissal and his or her call time the next day. For a producer, this term refers to a place in "development hell" where the deal for his picture has been bought by someone else who, undoubtedly, will have a whole new set of demands.

Two-shot: A medium shot showing two characters from the waist up.

Type: By this author's definition, the physical "look" of an actor based on gender, age, ethnic/cultural origin, and occupation. See the section An Actor Prepares.

Typecasting: Casting a role based on physical appearance more than on acting skill.

Under five (U-5): In an AFTRA contract, a principal role which has less than five lines.

Understudy: An actor hired to perform a role if the principal actor hired to do so cannot perform it.

Upstage: The area at the back of the stage, away from the audience. Downstage is toward the audience. Stages at one time were raked so that the back really was higher. This allowed characters upstage to be seen from the audience, which for centuries was seated in a level area. Eventually, someone got the fine idea to switch this situation around.

Upgrade: Promotion from an extra to a principal.

Use Cycle: The thirteen week period during which a commercial is actually used, or aired, as opposed to a holding cycle, which has different contractual provisions.

Voice Over (VO): An audio recording where the actor is heard but not seen.

Waivers: Board-approved exceptions to union contracts.

Walk-on: A real small role where you walk off real soon after you walk on.

Walla Walla: Fake background noise to simulate crowd mutterings. The words "rhubarb" and "plastic avocado," are also used.

Wardrobe: Both the costumes or clothes an actor wears, and the place where he goes to get them and later to turn them back in.

Wardrobe Allowance: Money you get paid, if you are a principal, for wearing your own stuff. Extras don't get paid for this unless it's formal wear.

Wardrobe Fitting: Going over to wardrobe to get your costume, then trying it on and letting them put pins in it where it needs to be altered. You get paid for this unless you are making above scale.

WGA: Writers Guild of America. The union for film and TV writers.

Wild Spot: The equivalent of syndication for commercials, ie commercials which are aired on a station-by-station agreement rather than aired on the networks.

Wild Track: An audio recording not made at the same time as a filmed sequence and not having a direct relationship to it.

Work Permit: Written permission to work, usually required for children and immigrants.

Wrap: The end of a day's work and/or the end of a production, especially the latter. The expression comes from wrapping up a can of shot film for shipment.

Zed Card: A modelling composite.

Zoom: A camera lens which can mechanically adjust from a close-up to a long shot and vice versa without moving the camera. "Zooming in" has the effect of making the object seem to rush to the audience, zooming out of making the audience "rocket away" from the object. The dolly shot has the opposite effect.

Talent Agents and Casting Directors

Regional Talent Agents

Arizona Agents

Act - Grissom Theatrical
6264 East Grant Road
Tucson AZ 85712
[602] 885-3246

Robert Black Agency
20 East University #306
Tempe, AZ 85281
[602] 966-2537

The Blue Ox Talent Agency
4130 North Goldwater Blvd. Suite 121
Scottsdale, AZ 85012
[602] 423-8669

Dani's Agency
1 East Camelback Road #550
Phoenix, AZ 85012
[602] 263-1918

Flair Agency
6700 North Oracle Road #501
Tucson, AZ 85704
[602] 742-1090

Fosi's Talent Agency
2777 North Campbell Avenue #209
Tucson, AZ 85719
[602] 795-3534

Leighton Agency, Inc.
3333 North 44th Street #2
Phoenix, AZ 85018
[602] 224-9255

Elizabeth Savage Talent, Inc.
4949 East Lincoln Drive #125
Paradise Valley, AZ 85253
[602] 840-3530

Signature Model & Talent Agency
20 East University #308
Tempe, AZ 85281
[602] 966-1102

California Agents

San Diego Area Agents:

Agency 2 Model & Talent Agency
2425 San Diego Avenue Suite 209
San Diego, CA 92110
[619] 291-9556

Andy Anderson Agency
7801 Mission Center Court
San Diego, CA 92108
[619] 294-4629

Artist Management Talent Agency
835 Fifth Avenue Suite 411
San Diego, CA 92101
[619] 233-6655

Elegance Talent Agency
2975 Madison Avenue
Carlsbad, CA 92008
[619] 434-3397

Liana Fields Talent Agency
2103 El Camino Real
Oceanside, CA 92054
[619] 433-6429

Beatrice Lily Talent Agency
1250 Prospect Street Suite 100
San Diego, CA 92037
[619] 454-3579

**Nouveau Model Management &
Talent Agency**
9823 Pacific Heights Blvd Suite M
San Diego, CA 92121
[619] 453-2727

Janice Patterson Talent Agency
2254 Moore Street Suite 104
San Diego, CA 92110
[619] 295-9477

143

Quantum Entertainment Talent Agency
3505 Camino Del Rio South, Suite 220
San Diego, CA 92108
[619] 528-8203

San Diego Model Management
824 Camino Del Rio North, Suite 552
San Diego, CA 92108
[619] 296-1018

Shamon Freitas & Company
2400 Kettner Boulevard Suite 212
San Diego, CA 92101
[619] 234-3043

San Francisco Area Agents

Covers Model & Talent Agency
2300 Bethards Drive Suite F
Santa Rosa, CA 95405
[707] 575-5224

Marla Dell Talent
1996 Union Street Suite 303
San Francisco, CA 94104
[415] 563-9213

Film Theatre Actors Exchange
582 Market Street Suite 302
San Francisco, CA 94104
[415] 433-3920

The Frazer Agency
4300 Stevens Creek Blvd Suite 126
San Jose, CA 95129
[408] 554-1055

Look Model & Talent Agency
166 Geary Blvd Suite 1406
San Francisco, CA 94108
[415] 781-2841

Los Latinos Talent Agency/Talent Plus
2801 Moorpark Avenue,
#11 Dyer Building
San Jose, CA 95128
[408] 296-2213

Mitchell Talent Management
323 Geary Street Suite 303
San Francisco, CA 94102
[415] 395-9291

The Panda Agency
3721 Hoen Avenue
Santa Rosa, CA 95405
[707] 576-0711

Quinn-Tonry, Inc.
601 Brannan Street
San Francisco, CA 94102
[415] 391-1800

San Francisco Top Models and Talent
870 Market Street Suite 1076
San Francisco, CA 94102
[415] 391-1800

Jennifer Spalding & Associates
1728 Union Street Suite 301
San Francisco, CA 94102
[415] 346-6177

The Stars Agency
777 Davis Street
San Francisco, CA 94111
[415] 421-6272

Los Angeles Area Agents

A S A
4430 Fountain Avenue Suite A
Los Angeles, CA 90029
[213] 662-9787

Abrams Artists & Associates
9200 Sunset Blvd. Suite 625
Los Angeles, CA 90069
[310] 859-0625

Abrams, Rubaloff & Lawrence
8075 West 3rd Street Suite 303
Los Angeles, CA 90048
[213] 935-1700

144

Acme Talent & Literary Agency
6310 San Vincente Blvd. Suite 520
Los Angeles, CA 90048
[213] 954-2263

Action Artists Agency
11020 Ventura Blvd. Suite E
Studio City, CA 91604
[818] 766-1026

AFH Management, Talent Agency
7819 Beverly Blvd.
Los Angeles CA 90036
[213] 658-9152

Agency For Performing Arts
9000 Sunset Blvd. Suite 1200
Los Angeles, CA 90069
[310] 273-0744

The Agency
10351 Santa Monica Blvd. Suite 211
Los Angeles, CA 90025
[310] 551-3000

Aimee Entertainment
13743 Victory Blvd.
Van Nuys, CA 91401
[818] 994-9354

Allen Talent Agency
11755 Wilshire Blvd. Suite 1750
Los Angeles, CA 90025
474-7524

Bonni Allen Talent
260 S. Beverly Drive
Beverly Hills, CA 90212
[310] 247-1865

Alliance Talent, Inc.
8949 Sunset Blvd. Suite 202
West Hollywood, CA 90069
[310] 858-1090

Carlos Alvarado Agency
8455 Beverly Blvd. Suite 406
Los Angeles, CA 90048
[213] 655-7978

Mortimer Ambrosio
9150 Wilshire Blvd. Suite 175
Beverly Hills, CA 90212
[310] 274-4274

Amsel, Eisenstadt & Frazier
6310 San Vincente Blvd. Suite 401
Los Angeles, CA 90048
[213] 939-1188

Angel City Talent
1680 Vine Street Suite 716
Los Angeles, CA 90028
[213] 463-1680

Chris Apodaca Agency
2049 Century Park East Suite 1200
Los Angeles, CA 90067
[310] 284-284-3484

Apodaca/Munro Talent Agency
13801 Ventura Blvd.
Sherman Oaks, CA 91423
[818] 380-2700

Irvin Arthur Associates LTD.
9363 Wilshire Blvd. Suite 212
Beverly Hills, CA 90210
[310] 278-5934

Artists Management Agency
4340 Campus Drive #210
Newport Beach, CA 92660
[714] 261-7557

Artists Network
12001 Ventura Place Suite 331
Studio City, CA 91604

Artists Agency
1000 Santa Monica Blvd. Suite 305
Los Angeles, CA 90067
[310] 277-7779

Artists First, Inc.
450 South Weverly Drive
Beverly Hills, CA 90211
[310] 550-8606

145

Artists Group, Ltd
1930 Century Park West Suite 403
Los Angeles, CA 90067
[310] 552-1100

Atkins and Associates
303 South Crescent Heights
Los Angeles, CA 90048
[213] 658-1025

B O P - LA Talent Agency
1467 North Tamarind Avenue
Los Angeles, CA 90028
[213] 466-8667

Badgley & Connor
9229 Sunset Boulevard
Suite 311
Los Angeles, CA 90069
[310] 278-9313

Baier-Kleinman International
3855 Lankershim Blvd.
North Hollywood, CA 91604
[818] 761-1001

Baldwin Talent, Inc.
500 Sepulveda Blvd. 4th Floor
Los Angeles, CA 90049
[310] 472-7919

Bobby Ball Talent Agency
8075 West 3rd Street Suite 550
Los Angeles, CA 90048
[213] 964-7300

Rickey Barr Talent Agency
1010 Hammond Suite 202
Los Angeles, CA
[310] 276-0887

Bauman, Hiller & Associates
5750 Wilshire Blvd. Suite 512
Los Angeles, CA 90036
[213] 857-6666

BDP & Associates Talent Agency
10637 Burbank Blvd.
North Hollywood, CA 91601
[818] 506-7615

Sara Bennet Agency
6404 Hollywood Blvd Suite 327
Los Angeles, CA 90028
[213] 965-9666

Lois J. Benson
8360 Melrose Avenue Suite 203
Los Angeles, CA 90069
[213] 653-0500

Marian Berzon Talent Agency
336 East 17th Street
Costa Mesa, CA 92627
[714] 631-5936

The Bigley Agency
6442 Coldwater Canyon Avenue Suite 211
North Hollywood, CA 91606
[818] 761-9971

Yvette Bikoff Agency, Ltd.
621 North Orlando Suite 8
West Hollywood, CA 90048
[213] 655-6123

Bonnie Black Talent Agency
4405 Riverside Drive Suite 305
Burbank, CA 91505
[818] 840-1299

The Blake Agency
415 North Camden Drive, Suite 121
Beverly Hills, CA 90210
[310]246-0241

Nina Blanchard
957 North Cole Avenue
Los Angeles, CA 90038
[213] 462-7274

J. Michael Bloom
9255 Sunset Blvd 7th Floor
Los Angeles, CA 90069
[310] 275-6800

Nicole Bordeaux Talent Agency
1503 North Gardner Suite 12
Los Angeles, CA 90046
[310] 289-2550

Borinstein Oreck Bogart
8271 Melrose Avenue Suite 110
Los Angeles, CA 90046
[213] 658-7500

Brand Model & Talent
17941 Skypark Circle Suite F
Irvine, CA 92714
[714] 251-0555

Paul Brandon & Associates
1033 North Carol Drive Suite T-6
Los Angeles, CA 90069
[310] 273-6173

S. W. Brandon's Commercials
Unlimited
9601 Wilshire Blvd.
Beverly Hills, CA 90210
[310] 888-8788

Bressler, Kelly & Kipperman
15760 Ventura Blvd. Suite 1730
Encino, CA 91436
[818] 905-1155

Alex Brewis Agency
12429 Laurel Terrace Drive
Studio City, CA 91604
[818] 509-0831

Jim Bridges Enterprises
5000 Lankershim Blvd. Suite 7
North Hollywood, CA 91601
[213] 962-6075

The Brustein Company
2644 30th Street 1st Floor
Santa Monica, CA 90405
[310] 452-3330

Don Buchwald & Associates
9229 Sunset Blvd.
West Hollywood, CA 90069
[310] 278-3600

Burkett Talent Agency
1700 East Garry Suite 113
Santa Ana, CA 92705
[714] 724-0465

Iris Burton Agency
1450 Belfast Drive
Los Angeles, CA 90069
[310] 652-0954

C La Vie Model & Talent
7507 Sunset Boulevard Suite # 201
Hollywood, CA 90046
[213] 969-0541

CL INC.
843 N. Sycamore Avenue
Hollywood, CA 90038
[213] 461-3971

CNA
1801 Avenue of the Stars, Suite 1250
Hollywood, CA 90067
[310] 556-4343

Cactus Talent Agency
13601 Ventura Boulevard, Suite #112
Sherman Oaks, CA 91423
[818] 986-7432

Camden-ITG
822 S. Robertson Boulevard, Suite 200
Hollywood, CA 90035
[310]289-2700

Barbara Cameron & Associates
8369 Sausalito Avenue #A
West Hills, CA 91304
[818] 888-6107

Capital Artists
8383 Wilshire Boulevard, Suite 954
Beverly Hills, CA 90211
[213] 658-8118

Career Artists International
11030 Ventura boulevard, Suite #3
Studio City, CA 91604
[818] 980-1315

Carglo Talent Agency
703 S. Glendora Avenue, Suite 6
West Covina, CA 91790
[213] 934-5259

William Carrol Agency
139 N San Fernando Rd., Suite A
Burbank, CA 91502
[818] 848-9948

Castle-Hill Talent Agency
1101 S. Orlando Avenue
Hollywood, CA 90035
[213] 653-3535

Cavaleri & Associates
6605 Hollywood Boulevard, Suite 220
Hollywood, CA 90028
[213] 683-1354

Century Artist, Ltd.
9744 Wilshire Boulevard, Suite 308
Beverly Hills, CA 90212
[310] 273-4366

The Chasin Agency
8899 Beverly Boulevard, Suite 713
Hollywood, CA 90048
[310] 278-7505

Chateau Billings Talent Agency
5657 Wilshire boulevard, Suite 340
Hollywood, CA 90036
[213] 965-5432

Jack Chutuk & Associates
2121 Avenue of the Stars, Suite 700
Hollywood, CA 90067
[310] 552-1773

Circle Talent Associates
433 N Camden Drive, Suite 400
Beverly Hills CA 90212
[310] 285-1585

W. Randolph Clark Company
2431 Hyperion Avenue
Hollywood, CA 90027
[213] 953-4960

Colleen Cler Modeling
120 S. Victory Boulevard, Suite 206
Burbank, CA 91502
[818] 841-7943

Coast to Coast Talent Group
4942 Vineland Avenue, Suite 200
N. Hollywood, CA 91601
[818] 762-6278

Colours Model & Talent Agency
7551 Melrose Avenue, Suite 6
Hollywood, CA 90046
[213] 658-7072

Contemporary Artists Ltd.
1427 Third Street Promenade, Suite 205
Santa Monica, CA 90401
[310] 395-1800

The Coppage Company
11501 Chandler Boulevard
N. Hollywood, CA 91601
[818] 980-1106

Coralie Jr. Theatrical Agency
4789 Vineland Avenue, Suite 100
N. Hollywood, CA 91602
[818] 766-9501

The Cosden Agency
3518 West Cahuenga Boulevard, Suite 216
Hollywood, CA 90068
[818] 752-4000

The Craig Agency
8485 Melrose Place, Suite E
Hollywood, CA 90069
[213] 655-0236

Creative Artists Agency
9830 Wilshire Boulevard
Beverly Hills, CA 90212
[310] 288-4545

Francis Creighton Agency
3441 West Cahuenga Boulevard
Hollywood, CA 90068
[213] 462-1566

Susan Crow & Associates
1010 Hammond Street, Suite 102
Wes Hollywood 90069
[310] 859-9784

Lil Cumber Attractions
6363 Sunset Boulevard, Suite 807
Hollywood, CA 90028
[213] 469-1919

Cunningham, Escott & Dipene
10635 Santa Monica Boulevard Suite 130
Hollywood, CA 90025
[313] 475-2111

DH Talent Agency
1800 N. Highland Avenue, Suite 300
Hollywood Avenue, CA 90028
[213] 962-6643

Dade-Schultz Associates
11846 Ventura Boulevard, Suite 201
Studio City, CA 91604
[818] 760-3100

Mary Webb Davis Talent Agency
515 N. La Cienaga Boulevard
Hollywood, CA 90048
[310] 652-6850

The Devroe Agency
6311 Romaine Street
Hollywood, CA 90038
[213] 962-3040

Durkin Artists
12229 Ventura Boulevard, Suite 202
Studio City, CA 91604
[818] 762-9936

Dytman & Schwartz Talent Agency
9200 Sunset Boulevard, Suite 809
Hollywood, CA 90069
[310] 274-8844

Efendi Talent Agency
6525 Sunset Boulevard, Suite 207
Hollywood, CA 90028
[213] 957-0006

Elite Model Management
345 n. Maple Drive, Suite 397
Beverly Hills, CA 90210
[310] 274-9395

Ellis Talent Group
6025 Sepulveda Boulevard, Suite 201
Van Nuys, CA 91411
[818] 997-7447

Emerald Artists
6565 Subset Boulevard, Suite 312
Hollywood, CA 90028
[310] 271-7120

Epstein-Wyckoff-Lamanna & Associates
280 S. Beverly Drive, Suite 400
Beverly Hills, CA 90212
[310] 278-7222

Estephan Talent Agency
6018 Greenmeadow Rd.
Lakewood, CA 90713
[310] 421-8048

FPA Talent Agency
12701 Moorpark, Suite 205
Studio City, CA 91604
[818] 508-6691

Eileen Farrell Talent Agency
10500 Magnolia Boulevard
N. Hollywood, CA 91601
[818] 831-7003

Favored Artists Agency
8150 Beverly Boulevard, Suite 201
Hollywood, CA 90048
[310] 247-1040

William Felber & Associates
2126 Cahuenga Boulevard
Hollywood, CA 90068
[213] 466-7629

Ferrar-Maziroff Associates
8430 Santa Monica Boulevard, Suite 220
Hollywood, CA 90069
[213] 654-2601

Lliana Fields Talent Agency
3325 Wilshire Boulevard, Suite 749
Hollywood, CA 90010
[213] 487-3656

Film Artists Associates
7080 Hollywood Boulevard, Suite 704
Hollywood, CA 90028
[213] 463-1010

First Artist AGENCY
10000 Riverside Drive, Suite 6
Toluca Lake, CA 91602
[818] 509-9292

Flick East & West Talents, Inc.
9057 Nemo Street, Suite A
West Hollywood, CA 90069
[310] 247-1777

Judith Fontaine Agency
9255 Sunset Boulevard
Hollywood, CA 90069
[213] 969-8398

Barry Freed Company
2029 Century Park East, Suite 600
Hollywood, CA 90067
[310] 277-1260

Fresh Model Management
6399 Wilshire Boulevard, Penthouse 7
Hollywood, CA 90048
[213] 651-5002

Alice Fries Agency
3210 Dewitt, Suite A
Hollywood, CA 90068
[213] 876-2990

Gage Group Inc.
9255 Sunset Boulevard, Suite 515
Hollywood, CA 90069
[310] 859-8777

Helen Garrett talent Agency
6525 Sunset Boulevard 5th Floor
Hollywood, CA 90028
[213]871-8707

Dale Garrick International
8831 Sunset Boulevard, Suite 408
Hollywood, CA 90069
[310] 657-2661

The Geddes Agency
1201 Green Acre Avenue
West Hollywood, CA 90046
[213] 878-1155

Laya Gelef Associates
16133 Ventura Boulevard, Suite 700
Encino, CA 91436
[818] 713-2610

Paul Gerard Agency
2918 Alta Vista Drive
Newport Beach, CA 92660
[714] 644-7950

Gerler-Stevens & Associates
3349 Cahuenga Boulevard West, Suite 1
Los Angelus, CA 90068
[213] 850-7386

The Gersh Agency
232 N Canon Drive
Beverly Hills, CA 90210
[310] 274-6611

Georgia Gilly
8721 Sunset Boulevard, Suite 103
Hollywood, CA 90069
[310] 657-5660

Gold, Marshak & Associates
3500 West Olive Avenue, Suite 1400
Burbank, CA 91505
[818] 972-4300

Goldley Company Inc.
116 N. Robertson Boulevard
Hollywood, CA 90048
[310] 657-3277

Gordon Company Talent Agency
12700 Ventura Boulevard, Suite 340
Studio city, CA 91604
[818] 907-0220

Michelle Gordon & Associates
260 S. Beverly Drive, Suite 308
Beverly Hills. CA 90212
[310] 246-9930

HWA Talent Representatives, Inc.
1964 Westwood Blvd. Suite 400
Los Angeles, CA 90025
[310] 446-1313

Buzz Halliday & Associates
8899 Beverly Blvd. Suite 620
Los Angeles, CA 90048
[310] 275-6028

Halpern & Associates
12304 Santa Monica Blvd. Suite 104
Los Angeles, CA 90025
[310] 571-4488

Mitchell J. Hamilburg Agency
292 South La Cienega #312
Beverly Hills, CA 90211
[310] 657-1501

Vaughn D. Hart & Associates
200 North Robertson Blvd Suite 219
Beverly Hills, CA 90211
[310] 273-7887

Headline Artists Agency
16400 Ventura Blvd Suite 324
Encino, CA 91436
[818] 986-1730

Beverly Hecht Agency
8949 Sunset Blvd. Suite 203
Los Angeles, CA 90069
[310] 278-3544

Henderson-Hogan Agency
247 South Beverly Drive
Beverly Hills, CA 90212
[310] 278-3544

Hervey-Grimes Talent Agency
14200 Ventura Blvd. Suite 109
Sherman Oaks, CA 91413
[818] 981-0891

House of Representatives Talent Agency
9911 Pico Blvd Suite 1060
Los Angeles, CA 90035
[310] 772-0772

Howard Talent West
12178 Ventura Blvd. Suite 201
Studio City, CA 91604
[818] 766-5300

Martin Hurwitz Associates
427 North Canon Drive Suite 215
Beverly Hills, CA 90210
[310] 274-0240

IFA Talent Agency
8730 Sunset Blvd. Suite 490
Los Angeles, CA 90069
[310] 659-5522

Image Talent Agency
8730 Sunset Blvd. Suite 490
Los Angeles, CA 90069
[310] 277-9134

Innervision Talent Agency
1901 Avenue of the Stars
Los Angeles, CA 90067
[310] 289-7918

Innovative Artists
1999 Avenue of the Stars
Los Angeles, CA 90067
[310] 289-7918

International Creative Management
8942 Wilshire Blvd.
Beverly Hills, CA 90211
[310] 550-4000

It Model Management
526 North Larchmont Blvd.
Los Angeles, CA 90004
[213] 962-9564

JWS Artist Agency
8489 West Third Street Suite 1092
Los Angeles, CA 90048
[213] 651-5010

Jackman & Taussig
1815 Butler Avenue Suite 120
Los Angeles, CA 90025
[310] 478-6641

George Jay Agency
6269 Selma Avenue #15
Los Angeles, CA 90028
[213] 465-0232

Thomas Jennings & Associates
28035 Dorothy Drive Suite 210A
Agoura, CA 91301
[818] 879-1260

Joseph, Heldfond & Rix
1717 North Highland Avenue Suite 414
Los Angeles, CA 90028
[213] 466-9111

The Kaplan-Stahler Agency
8383 Wilshire Blvde
Beverly Hills, CA 90211
[213] 653-4483

Karg, Weissenbach & Associates
329 N. Wetherly Drive # 101
Beverly Hills, CA 90210
[310] 205-0435

Kelman-Arletta
7813 Sunset Boulevard
Hollywood, CA 90046
[213] 851-8822

Kerwin-Williams Agency
1605 N. Cahuenga Boulevard, Suite 202
Hollywood, CA 90028
[213] 469-5155

Taylor Kjar Agency
10653 Riverside Drive
Toluca Lake, CA 91602
[818] 760-0321

Eric Klass Agency
144 S. Beverly Drive # 405
Beverly Hills, CA 90212
[310] 274-9169

Paul Kohner Inc.
9169 Sunset Boulevard
Hollywood, CA 90069
[310] 550-1060

Victor Kruglov & Associates
7060 Hollywood Boulevard, Suite 1220
Hollywood, CA 90028
[213] 957-9000

Krups Talent Agency
11950 Ventura Boulevard
Studio City, CA 91604
[800] 995-7877

L.A. Talent
8335 Sunset Boulevard, 2nd Floor
Hollywood, CA 90069
[213] 656-3722

L.A. Artists
2566 Overland Avenue, Suite 550
Hollywood, CA 90064
[310] 202-0254

Stacey Lane Talent Agency
13455 Ventura Boulevard, Suite 240
Sherman Oaks, CA 91423
[818] 501-2668

The Lawrence Agency
3575 Cahuenga Boulevard, West
Suite 125-3, Hollywood, CA 90068
[213] 851-7711

Guy Lee & Associates
4150 Riverside Drive, Suite 212
Burbank, CA 91505
[818]848-7475

Lenhoff-Robinson Talent
& Literary Agency
1728 S. La Cienaga Boulevard
Hollywood, CA 90035
[310] 558-4700

The Levin Agency
9255 Sunset boulevard # 401
West Hollywood, CA 90069
[310] 278-0353

Terry Lichtman Co.
4439 Worster Avenue
Studio City, CA 91604
[818] 783-3003

Robert Light Agency
6404 Wilshire Boulevard, Suite 900
Hollywood, CA 90048
[213] 651-1777

Linder & Associates
2049 Century Park East, Suite 2750
Hollywood, CA 90067
[310] 277-9223

The Loft Agency
369 S. Dohney Drive, Suite 203
Beverly Hills, CA 90211
[310] 576-9012

Los Angeles Premiere Artists Agency
8899 Beverly Boulevard, Suite 102
Hollywood, CA 90048
[310] 271-1414

Los Angeles Sports
2121 Avenue of the Stars, 6the Floor
Hollywood, CA 90067
[213] 654-4880

Lovell & Associates
1350 N. Highland Avenue
Hollywood, CA 90028

Lynne & Reilly Agency
Toluca Plaza Building
6735 Forest Lawn Drive, Suite 313
Hollywood, CA 90068
[213] 850-1984

MGA/Mary Grady Agency
150 E Olive Avenue, Suite 304
Burbank, CA 91502
[818] 766-4414

Mademoiselle Talent Agency
8693 Wilshire Boulevard, Suite 200
Beverly Hills, CA 90211
[310] 289-8005

Major Clients Agency
2121 Avenue of the Stars
Hollywood, CA 90067
[310] 284-6400

Alese Marshall Model &
Commercial Agency
23900 Hawthorne Boulevard, Suite 100
Torrance, CA 90505
[310] 378-1223

The Martel Agency
1680 N. Vine Street #203
Hollywood, CA 90028
[213] 461-5943

Maxine's Talent Agency
4830 Encino Avenue
Encino, CA 91316
[818] 986-986-2946

Media Artist's Group
8383 Wilshire Blvd Suite 954
Beverly Hills, CA 90211
[213] 658-5050

Metropolitan Talent Agency
4526 Wilshire Blvd
Los Angeles, CA 90010
[213]857-4500

Miramar Talent Agency
9157 Sunset Blvd Suite 300
Los Angeles, CA 90069
[310] 858-1900

The Mishkin Agency
2355 Benedict Canyon Drive
Beverly Hills, CA 90210
[310] 274-5261

Patty Mitchell Agency
11425 Moorpark Street
Studio City, CA 91602
[818] 508-6181

Moore Artists Talent Agency
1551 South Robertson Blvd
Los Angeles, CA 90035
[310] 274-7451

William Morris Agency
151 El Camino Drive
Beverly Hills, CA 90212
[310] 274-7451

H. David Moss & Associates
733 North Seward Street
Los Angeles, CA 90038
[213] 465-1234

Mary Murphy Agency
6014 Greenbush Avenue
Van Nuys, CA 91401
[818] 989-6076

Susan Nathe & Associates
8281 Melrose Avenue Suite 200
Los Angeles, CA 90046
[213] 653-7573

Omnipop Inc.
10700 Ventura Blvd
Studio City, CA 91604
[818] 980-9267

Orange Grove Group, Inc.
12178 Ventura Blvd. Suite 205
Studio City, CA 91604
[818] 762-7498

Cindy Oshbrink Talent Agency
4605 Lankershim Blvd. Suite 401
North Hollywood, CA 91602
[818] 760-2488

Dorothy Day & Associates
13223 Ventura Blvd. Suite F
Studio City, CA 91604
[818] 905-9510

Pakula King & Associates
9229 Sunset Blvd. Suite 315
Los Angeles, CA 90069
[310] 281-4868

Paradigm Talent Agency
10100 Santa Monica Blvd. Suite 2500
Los Angeles, CA 90067
[310] 277-4400

Paragon Talent Agency, Inc.
8439 Sunset Blvd. Suite 301
Los Angeles, CA 90069
[213] 654-4554

The Partos Company
3630 Barham Blvd. #Z108
Los Angeles, CA 90068
[213] 876-5500

Perseus Modeling & Talent
3807 Wilshire Blvd. Suite 1102
Los Angeles, CA 90010
[213] 383-2322

Players Talent Agency
8770 Shoreham Drive Suite 2
West Hollywood, CA 90069
[310] 289-8777

Premier Talent Agency
2001 Wilshire Blvd 6th Floor
Santa Monica, CA 90403
[310] 882-6900

Prima Model Management, Inc.
933 North La Brea Avenue Suite 200
Los Angeles, CA 90038
[213] 882-6900

Privilege Talent Agency
8170 Beverly Blvd. Suite 204
Los Angeles, CA 90048
[213] 658-8781

Pro-Sport & Entertainment Co.
1990 South Bundy Drive Suite 700
Los Angeles, CA 90025
[310] 207-0228

Progressive Artists
400 South Beverly Drive, Suite 216
Beverly Hills, CA 90212
[310] 553-8561

Gordon Rael Company
9255 Sunset Blvd. Suite 425
Los Angeles, CA 90069
[213] 969-8483

Renaissance Talent & Literary Agency
152 North La Peer Drive
Los Angeles, CA 90048
[310] 289-3636

Stephanie Rogers & Associates
3575 West Cahuenga Blvd. Suite 249
Los Angeles, CA 90068
[213] 851-5155

Cindy Romano Modeling
& Talent Agency
266 South Palm Canyon Drive
Palm Springs, CA 92262
[619] 323-3333

Gilla Roos West LTD.
9744 Wilshire Blvd suite 203
Beverly Hills, CA 90212
[310] 274-653-7383

The Marion Rosenberg Office
8428 Melrose Place Suite B
Los Angeles, CA 90069
[213] 653-7383

Natalie Rosson Agency
11712 Moorpark Street Suite 204
Studio City, CA 91604
[818] 508-1445

SDB Partners, Inc.
1801 Avenue of the Stars Suite 902
Los Angeles, CA 90067
[310] 785-0060

The Sanders Agency
8831 Sunset Blvd. # 304
Los Angeles, CA 90069
[310] 652-1119

Sarnoff Company Inc.
3900 West Alameda Avenue
Burbank, CA 91505
[818] 972-1779

The Savage Agency
6212 Banner Avenue
Los Angeles, CA 90038
[818] 461-8316

Jack Scagnetti Talent Agency
5118 Vineland Avenue Suite 102
North Hollywood, CA 91601
[818] 762-3871

The Irv Schechter Company
9300 Wilshire Blvd. #410
Beverly Hills, CA 90212
[310] 278-8070

Shiowitz, Clay, Rose, Inc.
1680 North Vine Street Suite 614
Los Angeles, CA 90028
[213] 650-7300

Sadie Schnarr Talent
8281 Melrose Avenue #200
Los Angeles, CA 90046
[213] 653-9479

Judy Schoen & Associates
606 North Larchmont Blvd. Suite 309
Los Angeles, CA 90004
[213] 962-1950

Don Schwartz Associates
8749 Sunset Blvd.
Los Angeles, CA 90069
[310] 657-8910

Screen Artists Agency
12435 Oxnard Street
North Hollywood, CA 91606
[818] 755-0026

Screen Children's Talent Agency
4000 Riverside Drive Suite A
Burbank, CA 91505
[818] 846-4300

Selected Artists Agency
3575 Cahuenga Blvd. West
Los Angeles, CA 90068
[818] 905-5744

Shapira & Associates
15301 Ventura Blvd. Suite 345
Sherman Oaks, CA 91403
[818] 906-0322

Shapiro-Lichtman, Inc.
8827 Beverly Blvd.
Los Angeles, CA 90048
[310] 859-8877

155

Lew Sherrell Agency
1354 Los Robles
Palm Springs, CA 92262
[619] 323-9514

Sherwood-Greene Talent Agency
223 1/2 Abalone Avenue
Balboa Island, CA 92662
[714] 675-4058

Showbiz Entertainment
6922 Hollywood Blvd. Suite 207
Los Angeles, CA 90028
[213] 469-9931

Dorothy Shreve Agency
2665 North Palm Canyon Drive
Palm Springs, CA 92262
[619] 327-5855

The Shumaker Talent Agency
6533 Hollywood Blvd. Suite 301
Los Angeles, CA 90028
[213] 464-0745

Jerome Siegal Associates
7551 Sunset Blvd. Suite 203
Los Angeles, CA 90046
[213] 850-1275

Sierra Talent Agency
14542 Ventura Blvd. Suite 207
Sherman Oaks, CA 91403
[818] 907-9645

Silver, Kass & Massetti Agency, Ltd.
8730 Sunset Blvd. Suite 480
Los Angeles, CA 90069
[310] 289-0909

Richard Sindell & Associates
8271 Melrose Avenue Suite 202
Los Angeles, CA 90046
[213 653-5051

Michael Slessinger Associates
8730 Sunset Blvd Suite 220
Los Angeles, CA 90069
[310] 657-7113

Susan Smith & Associates
121 San Vincente Blvd.
Beverly Hills, CA 90211
[213] 852-4777

Camille Sorice Talent Agency
16661 Ventura Blvd. Suite 400-E
Encino, CA 91436
[818] 995-1775

Special Artists Agency
335 North Maple Drive Suite 360
Beverly Hills, CA 90210
[310] 859-9688

Specialty Models
8609 Sherwood Drive
West Hollywood, CA 90069
[310] 657-5367

Star Talent Agency
4555 1/2 Mariotta Avenue
Toluca Lake, CA 91602
[818] 509-1931

Starwil Talent Agency
6253 Hollywood, Blvd. # 730
Los Angeles, CA 90028
[213] 874-1239

Charles H. Stern Agency
11755 Wilshire Blvd. Suite 2320
Los Angeles, CA 90025
[310] 479-1788

Steven R. Stevens Talent Agency
3518 West Cahuenga Blvd. Suite 301
Los Angeles, CA 90068
[213] 850-5761

Stone Manners Agency
8091 Selma Avenue
Los Angeles, CA 90046
[213] 654-7575

Sutton, Barth & Vennari Inc.
145 South Fairfax Avenue Suite 310
Los Angeles, CA 90036
[213] 938-6000

Talent Group, Inc.
9250 Wilshire Blvd. suite 208
Beverly Hills, CA 90212
[310] 273-9559

Talon Theatrical Agency
567 South Lake
Pasadena, CA 91101
[818] 577-1998

Tannen & Associates
1800 North Vine Street Suite 120
Los Angeles, CA 90028
[213] 466-6191

Thomas-Rossan Agency
124 South Lasky Drive
Beverly Hills, CA 90212
[310] 247-2727

Arlene Thornton & Associates
5657 Wilshire Blvd Suite 290
Los Angeles, CA 90036
[213] 939-5757

Tisherman Agency, Inc
6767 Forest Lawn Drive Suite 101
Los Angeles, CA 90068
[213] 850-6767

Tobias-Skouras & Associates
1015 Gayley Avenue suite 301
Los Angeles, CA 90024
[310] 208-2100

Total Acting Experience
20501 Venture Blvd Suite 112
Woodland Hills, CA 91364
[818] 340-9249

The Turtle Agency
12456 Ventura Blvd Suite 1
Studio City, CA 91604
[818] 506-6898

Twentieth Century Artists
15315 Magnolia Blvd. Suite 429
Sherman Oaks, CA 91403
[818] 884-5516

Umoja Talent Agency
2069 West Slauson Avenue
Los Angeles, CA 90047
[213] 290-6612

United Talent Agency, Inc.
9560 Wilshire Blvd. 5th Floor
Beverly Hills, CA 90212
[310] 273-6700

Erika Wain Agency
1418 North Highland Avenue #102
Los Angeles, CA 90028
[213] 460-4224

Wallis Agency
1126 Hollywood Way Suite 203-A
Burbank, CA 91505
[818] 953-4848

Curry Walls & Associates
9107 Wilshire Blvd. Suite #602
Beverly Hills, CA 90210
[310] 858-0085

Sandra Watt & Associates
7551 Melrose Avenue Suite 5
Los Angeles, CA 90046
[213] 851-1021

Ann Waugh Talent Agency
4731 Laurel Canyon Blvd. Suite 5
North Hollywood, CA 91607
[213] 851-1021

Ruth Webb Enterprises
7500 Devista Drive
Los Angeles, CA 90046
[213] 874-1700

West Model Management
& Talent Agency
7276 1/2 Melrose Avenue
Los Angeles, CA 90046
[213] 525-3355

The Whitaker Agency
12725 Ventura Blvd. Suite F
Studio City, CA 91604
[818] 766-4441

Shirley Wilson & Associates
5410 Wilshire Blvd. Suite 227
Los Angeles, CA 90036
[213] 857-6977

Ted Witzer Agency
6310 San Vincente Blvd. Suite 407
Los Angeles, CA 90048
[310] 553-9521

World Class Sorts
9171 Wilshire Blvd. # 404
Beverly Hills, CA 90210
[310] 278-2010

World-Wide Acts Talent Agency
7226 Leota Lane
Canoga Park, CA 91304
[818] 3408151

Carter Wright Enterprises
6533 Hollywood Blvd. Suite 201
Los Angeles, CA 90028
[213] 469-0944

Writers and Artists Agency
924 Westwood Blvd. Suite 900
Los Angeles, CA 90024
[310] 824-6300

Stella Zadeh & Associates
11759 Iowa Avenue
Los Angeles, CA 90025
[310] 207-4114

Zealous Artists, Inc.
139 South Beverly Drive Suite 222
Beverly Hills, CA 90212
[310] 281-3533

Colorado Agents

Donna Baldwin Talent
50 S. Steele Street #260
Denver, CO 80209
[303] 320-0067

Barbizon Talent Agency
7535 East Hampden Avenue #108
Denver, CO 80231
[303] 337-7954

J.F. Talent Inc.
5161 East Arapahoe Road #400
Littleton, CO 80122
[303] 771-4820

Looks Agency
3600 South Beeler Suite 310
Denver, CO 80237
[303] 740-2224

Voice Choice
1805 South Bellaire Street #130
Denver, CO 80222
[303] 756-9055

Looks Agency
202 East Cheyenne Mountain Blvd.
Suite N
Colorado Springs, CO 80906
[719] 527-9972

Florida Agents

Central Florida Agents

Berg Talent Agency
1115 N. Himes Avenue
Tampa, FL 33607
[813] 877-5533

Dott Burns Talent Agency
478 Severn
Tampa, FL 33606
[813] 251-5882

Bailey Talent Group
513 West Colonial Drive #6
Orlando, FL 32804
[407] 423-7872

158

Dimensions III Model & Talent
5205 South Orange Avenue #209
Orlando, FL 32809
[407] 851-2575
Suzanne Haley Talent
618 Wymore Road #2
Winter Park, FL 32789-2862
[407] 644-0600
Hurt-Garver Talent
400 North New York Avenue #207
Winter Park, FL 33844
[407] 740-5700
Strictly Speaking, Inc.
711 Executive Drive
Winter Park, Fl 32789
[407] 645-2111
Take 1 Employment Guild, Inc.
3800 South Tamiami Trail, Suite 318
Sarasota, FL 34239
[813] 364-9285

South Florida Agents

Act 1
1205 Washington Avenue
Miami Beach, FL 33139
[305] 672-0200
Coconut Grove Talent
3525 Vista Court
Miami, FL 33133
[305] 858-3002
Ada Gordon Talent
1995 N.E. 150th Street #C
North Miami, FL 33181
[305] 940-1311

Green & Green Model
& Talent Agency
1688 Meridian Avenue #802
Miami Beach, FL 31139
[305] 899-9953
Marbea Talent Agency
1946 N.E. 149th Street
Miami, FL 33181
[305] 949-0615
Miami Talent Inc.
278 South University Drive
Plantation, FL 33324
[305] 472-1707
Marion Polan Talent Agency
10 N.E. 11th Avenue
Ft. Lauderdale, FL 33139
[305] 379-7526
Michele Pomier Models
81 Washington Avenue
Miami Beach, FL 33139
[305] 672-9344
Rocki Talent Agency
12100 N.E. 16th Avenue #202
N. Miami, FL 33161
[305] 899-9150
Stellar Talent Agency
505 Lincoln Road #101
Miami Beach, FL 33139
[305] 672-2217

Georgia Agents

The Arnold Agency
P.O. Box 11528
Atlanta, GA 30355
[404] 279-9850
Atlanta Models & Talent
3030 Peachtree Road, NW # 660
Atlanta, GA 30305
[404] 261-9627

Bordon & Associates, LTD.
P.O. Box 11590
Atlanta, GA 30355
[404] 266-0664

The Burns Agency (GA)
602 Hammet Drive
Decatur, GA 30032
[404] 2998114

Genesis Model and Talent
1465 Northside Drive # 120
Atlanta, GA 30318
[404] 874-6448

Arlene Wilson, Inc.
887 West Marietta Street # N-101
Atlanta, GA 30318
[404] 876-8555

Hawaii Agents

ADR Model & Talent Agency
431 Kuwili Street
Honolulu, HI 96817
[808] 524-4777

Amos Kotomori Talent Services
1018 Hoawa Lane
Honolulu HI 96826
[808] 955-6511

Kathy Muller Agency
619 Kapahula Avenue
Penthouse
Honolulu HI 96815
[808] 737-7917

Illinois Agents

Chicago Agents

A-Plus Talent Agency Corporation
108 West Oaks Street
Chicago, IL 60610
[312] 642-8151

Ambassador Talent Agents, Inc.
333 North Michigan Avenue
Suite 314
Chicago, IL 60601

Aria Model & Talent Management, LTD
1017 West Washington, Suite 2A
Chicago, IL 60607
[213] 243-9400

Cunningham, Escott, Dipene
& Associates
676 St. Clair Street # 1900
Chicago, IL 60611-2922
[312] 280-5155

David & Lee
70 West Hubbard Street #200
Chicago, IL 60610
[312] 67-4444

Harise Davidson & Associates
60 East Wacker Place #2401
Chicago, IL 60601
[312] 782-4480

ETA Inc.
7558 South Chicago Avenue
Chicago, IL 60619
[312] 752-3955

Geddes Agency
1925 North Clybourn #402
Chicago, IL 60614
[312] 348-3333

Shirley Hamilton Agency Inc.
3333 East Ontario, Suite B
Chicago, IL 60610
[312] 787-4700

Jefferson & Associates, Inc. (IL)
1050 N. State
Chicago, IL 60610
[312] 337-1930

Susanne's A-Plus Talent
108 West Oak Street
Chicago, IL 60610
[310] 943-8315

160

Lily & Maureen's Talent Agency
5962 North Elston
Chicago, IL 60646
[312] 698-6364
Linda Jack Talent
230 East Ohio #200
Chicago, IL 60611
[312] 587-1155
Emilia Lorence, Ltd.
619 North Wabash
Chicago, IL 60611
[312] 787-2033
Nouvelle Talent Management
P.O. Box 578100
Chicago, IL 60657
[312] 944-1133
Phoenix Talent, Ltd.
410 South Michigan Avenue
Penthouse
Chicago, IL 60604
[312] 786-2024
Salazar & Navas Inc.
367 W. Chicago Avenue Suite 200
Chicago, IL 60610
[312] 751-3419
SA-RAH Talent Agency
1935 South Halsted Street #301
Chicago, IL 60608
[312] 733-2822
Stewart Talent Management Corporation
212 West Superior # 406
Chicago, IL 60610
[312] 943-3226
Voices Unlimited Inc.
680 North Lake Shore Drive #1330
Chicago, IL 60611
[312] 642-3262
Arlene Wilson Talent (IL)
430 West Erie #210
Chicago, IL 60610
[312] 573-0200

Other Illinois Agencies

North Shore Talent
450 Peterson Road
Libertyville, IL 60040
[708] 816-1811
Norman Shucart Enterprises
1417 Green Bay Road
Highland Park, IL 60035
[708] 433-1113
Howard Shultz
241 Golf Mill Center #328
Niles, IL 60714
[312] 867-4282

Indiana Agents

Act 1 Agency
6100 North Keystone
Indianapolis, IN 46220
[317] 255-3100
C.J. Mercury, Inc.
1330 Lake Avenue
Whiting, IN 46394
[219] 659-2701
Helen Wells Agency
11711 North Meridan Street #460
Carmel, IN 46032
[317] 843-5363

Kansas Agents

The Agency Models and Talent
3025 Mirriam Lane
Kansas City, KS 66106
[913] 362-8382
Hoffman International
10540 Marty #100
Overland Park, KS 66212
[913] 642-1060

Maggie Inc.
35 Newbury Street
Boston, MA 02210
[617] 536-2639
Models Group
374 Congress Street #305
Boston, MA 02210
[617] 4264711
Models, Inc.
218 Newbury Street
Boston MA 02116
[617] 437-6212

Michigan Agents

Affiliated Models Inc.
Affiliated Building
1680 Crooks Road
Troy, MI 48084
[810] 224-8770
C.L.A.S.S. Modeling & Talent Agency
1625 Haslet Road
Haslett, MI 48840
[313] 339-2777
Michael Jeffrys Agency
202 East Washington Suite 210
Ann Arbor, MI 48104
[313] 663-6398
Pastiche Models Inc.
1514 Wealthy Street S.E. #280
Grand Rapids MI 49506
[616] 451-2181
Powers Models & Talent Agency
16250 Northland Drive #239
Southfield, MI 48075
[313] 569-2247

Productions Plus
30600 Telegraph Road #2156
Birmingham, MI 48025-4532
[313] 644-5566
The Talent Shop
30100 Telegraph Road 3116
Birmingham, MI 48025
[313] 644-4877
Wayman Talent Agency
1959 East Jefferson 34H
Detroit, MI 48207
[313] 393-8300

Minnesota Agents

Caryn Models & Talent
63 South Ninth Street Suite 201
Minneapolis, MN 55402
[612] 338-0102
Creative Casting Inc.
860 Lumber Exchange Building
10 South 5th Street
Minneapolis, MN 55402
[612] 375-0525
Meredith Models Management
555 Fort Road #300
St. Paul, MN 55102
[612] 298-9555
The Eleanor Moore Agency
1610-B West Lake Street
Minneapolis, MN 55408
[612] 827-3823
New Faces Models & Talent Inc.
5217 Wayzata Blvd. #210
Minneapolis, MN 55416
[612] 544-8668
Susan Wehmann Models
1128 Harmon Place #205
Minneapolis, MN 55403
[612] 333-6393

162

Kansas City, MO, Agents

Model and Talent Managment
4528 Main Street
Kansas City Mo 64111
[816] 561-9967
MTC - Model, Talent, Charm LTD
4032 Broadway
Kansas City MO 64111
[816] 531-0333
Talent Unlimited
4049 Pennsylvania Avenue #300
Kansas City, MO 64111
[816] 561-9040

St. Louis Agents

The Delcia Agency
7201 Delmar
St. Louis, Mo 63130
[314] 726-3223
Model Management Agency Inc.
11815 Manchester Road
St. Louis, MO 63131
[314] 965-3264
Prima Models
710 North 2nd Street South
St. Louis, MO 63102
[314] 436-7705
The Quinn Agency
1062 Madison Street
St. Charles, MO 63108
[314] 947-0120
Talent Plus Inc.
55 Maryland Plaza
St. Louis, MO 63108
[314] 367-5588

The Talent Source Inc.
419 South Euclid
St. Louis, MO 63108
[314] 367-8585

New York Agents

Abrams Artists & Associates
420 Madison Avenue, 14th Floor New
York, NY 10017
[212] 935-8980
The Actors Group Agency
157 West 57th Suite 604
New York, Ny 10019
[212] 245-2930
Bret ADAMS Ltd
448 West 44th Street,
New York, Ny 10036
[212] 765-5630
Agency for Performing Arts
888 Seventh Avenue 6th Floor
New York, NY 10106
[212] 582-1500
Agents for the Arts, Inc.
203 West 23rd Steet, 3rd Floor
New York, NY 10011
[212] 229-2562
Alliance Talent Incorporated
1501 Broadway Suite 404
New York, NY 10036
[212] 840-6868
Michael Amato Theatrical Enterprises
1650 Broadway Suite 307
New York, NY 10019
[212] 247-4456
Ambrosio-Mortimer & Associates
165 West 46th Street Suite 1109
New York, NY 10036
[212] 719-1677

163

American International Talent
303 West 42nd Street Suite 608
New York, NY 10036
[212] 245-8888

Beverly Aanderson Agency
1501 Broadway Suite 2008
New York, NY 10036
[212] 944-7773

Andreadis Talent Agency, Inc.
119 West 57th Street Suite 711
New York, NY 10019
[212] 315-0303

Artist's Agency Inc.
230 West 55th Steet Suite 29D
New York, NY 10019
[212] 245-6960

Artist & Audience Entertainment
83 Riverside Drive
New York, NY 10024
[212] 72l-2400

Artist's Group East
1650 Broadway Suite 711
New York, Ny 10019
[212] 586-1452

Associated Booking Corporation
1995 Broadway
New York, NY l0023
[2l2] 874-2400

Richard Astor Agency
250 West 57th Street Suite 2014
New York, NY 10107
[212] 581-1970

Avenue Talent Ltd.
315 West 35th Street Suite 12B
New York, NY 10001
[212] 972-9040

Carol Baker Agency
165 West 46th Street Suite 1106
New York, NY 10036
[212] 719-4013

Barry, Haft, Brown Artists
165 West 46th Street
New York, NY 10036
[212] 869-9310

Bauman, Hiller & Associates
250 West 57th Street Suite 2223
New York, NY 10107
[212] 757-0098

Peter Beilin Agency
230 Park Avenue Suite 1223
New York, NY 10169
[212] 949-9119

Bethel Agency
641 West 59th Street Suite 116
New York 10019
[212] 664-0455

J. Michael Bloom & Associates
233 Park Avenue South 10th Floor
New York, NY 10003
[212] 529-6500

Bookers Inc.
150 Fifth Avenue Suite 834
New York, NY 645-9706
[212] 645-9706

Don Buchwald & Associates
10 East 44th Street
New York, NY 10017
[212] 861-1070

The Carry Company
1501 Broadway Suite 1408
New York, NY 10036
[212] 768-2793

The Carson Organization, Ltd
240 West 44th Street Penthouse 12
New York, NY 10036
[212] 221-1517

Carson/Adler Agency, Inc.
250 West 57th Street Suite 729
New York, NY 10107
[212] 307-1882

Richard Cataldi Agency
180 7th Avenue Suite 1C
New York, NY 10011
[212] 741 -7450

Coleman-Rosenberg
210 East 58th Street Suite 2F
New York, NY 10022
[212] 838-0734

Bill Cooper Associates, Inc.
224 West 49th Street Suite 411
New York, NY 10019
[212] 307-1100

Cunningham-Escott-Dipine
118 East 25th Street 6th Floor
New York, NY 10010
[212] 477-1666

Ginger Dicce Talent Agency, Inc.
1650 Broadway Suite 714
New York, NY 10019
[212] 474-7455

Douglas, Gorman, Rothacker
& Wilhelm, Inc.
1501 Broadway Suite 703
New York, NY 10036
[212] 382-2000

David Drummond Talent
Representatives
21 Pomander Walk
New York, NY 10025
[212] 877-6753

Duva-Flack Associates, Inc.
200 West 57th Street Suite 1407
New York, NY 10019
[212] 957-9600

Eastwood Talent Group, Inc
214 East 9th Street
New York, NY 10003
[212] 982-9700

Dulcina Eisen Associates
154 East 61st Street
New York, NY 10036
[212] 355-6617

Epstein, Wyckoff & Associates
311 West 43rd Street Suite 401
New York, NY 10036
[212] 586-9110

E. W. Flick Talents, Inc
881 7th Avenue Suite 1110
New York, NY 10019
[212] 307-1850

Frontier Booking International
1560 Broadway Suite 1110
New York, NY 10036
[212] 221-0220

The Gage Group, Inc.
315 West 57th Street Suite 4H
New York, NY 10019
[212] 541-5250

Gersh Agency New York, Inc.
130 West 42nd Street
New York, NY 10036
[212] 997-1818

Gilchrist Talent Group
310 Madison Avenue Suite 1025
New York, NY 10017
[212] 692-9166

H W A Talent Representatives
36 East 22nd Street 3rd Floor
New York, NY 10010
[212] 529-4555

Peggy Hadley Enterprises LTD
250 West 57th Street
New York, NY 10019
[212] 246-2166

Michael Hartig Agency Ltd.
156 5th Avenue Suite 820
New York, NY 10010
[212] 929-1772

Henderson-Hogan Agency Inc.
850 Seventh Avenue Suite 1003
New York, NY 10019
[212] 765-5190

Hodges Talent Agency Inc.
156 5th Avenue Suite 515
New York, NY 10010
[212] 691-2756

Barbara Hogenson Agency Inc.
2211 Broadway Suite 9B
New York, NY 10024
[212] 580-3293

Ingber & Associates
274 Madison Avenue Suite 1104
New York, NY 10024
[212] 889-9450

Innovative Artists Talent
& Literary Agency
1776 Broadway Suite 1810
New York, NY 10019
[212] 315-4455

International Creative Management
40 West 57th Street
New York, NY 10019
[212] 556-5600

It Models-Omars Men
251 5th Avenue 7th Floor Penthouse
New York, NY 10016
[212] 481-7220

Jam Theatrical Agency, Inc.
352 Seventh Avenue Suite 1500
New York, NY 10001
[212] 376-6330

Jan J. Agency
365 West 34th Street
New York, NY 10001
[212] 967-5265

Jordan, Gill & Dornbaum
Talent Agency
156 5th Avenue Suite 711
New York, NY 10010
[212] 463-8455

Charles Kerin Inc.
360 East 65th Street Suite 11J
New York, NY 10021
[212] 288-6111

Archer King
10 Columbus Circle Suite 1492
New York, NY 10019
[212] 765-3103

KMA Associates
211 West 56th Street Suite 17D
New York, NY 10019
[212] 581-4610

The Krasny Office Inc.
1501 Broadway Suite 1510
New York, NY 10036
[212] 730-8160

Lally Talent Agency
630 Ninth Avenue
New York, NY 10036
[212] 974-8718

Lantz Office
888 Seventh Avenue
New York, NY 10106
[212] 586-0200

Larner Lionel Ltd.
130 West 57th Street
New York, NY 10019
[212] 246-3105

Bruce Levy Agency
335 West 38th Street Suite 802
New York, NY 10018
[212] 563-7079Lure International Talent
Group Inc.
915 Broadway Suite 1210
New York, NY 10010
[212] 260-9300

Madison Talent Group Inc.
310 Madison Avenue Suite 1508
New York, NY 10017
[212] 922-9600

William Morris Agency Inc.
1350 Avenue of the Americas
New York, NY 10019
[212] 586-5100

Nouvelle Talent Management Inc.
20 Bethune Street Suite 3B
New York, NY 10014
[214] 645-0940

Omnipop Inc.
55 West Old Country Road
Hicksville, NY 11801
[516] 937-6011

Openheim/Christie Associates Ltd.
13 East 37th Street
New York, NY 10016
[212] 213-4330

Fifi Oscard Agency Inc.
24 West 40th Street Suite 17
New York, NY 10018
[212] 764-1100

Harry Packwood Talent Agency Ltd.
250 West 57th Street, Suite 2012
New York, NY 10107
[212] 586-8900

Dorothy Palmer Talent Agency
235 West 56th Street 24k
New York, NY 10019
[212] 765-4280

Paradigm Talent Agency
200 West 57th Street Suite 900
New York, NY 10019
[212] 246-1030

Pauline's Talent Corporation
379 West Broadway Suite 502
New York, NY 10012
[212] 941 6000

Premier Talent Associates
3 East 54th Street
New York, NY 10022
[212] 758-4900

Professional Artists Unlimited
513 West 54th Street
New York, NY 10019
[212] 247-8770

Pyrimid Entertainment Group
89 Fifth Avenue
New York, NY 10003
[212] 242-7274

Radioactive Talent Inc.
240-03 Linden Blvd.
Elmont, NY [11003]
[212] 315-1919

Norman Reich Agency
1650 Broadway Suite 303
New York, NY 10019
[212] 399-2881

Gilla Roos Ltd.
16 West 22nd Street 7th Floor
New York, NY 10010
[212] 727-7820

Sames & Rollnick Associates
250 West 57th Sueet Suite 703
New York, NY 10107
[212] 315-4434

The Sanders Agency Ltd.
1204 Broadway Suite 306
New York, NY 10001
[212] 779-3737

Schiffman, Ekman, Morrison, and Marx
22 West 19th Street 8th Floor
New York, NY 10011
[212] 627-5500

William Schill Agency
250 West 57th Street Suite 1429
New York, NY 10107
[212] 315-5919

Shuller Talent, Inc. AKA New York Kids
276 5th Avenue 10th Floor
New NY 10001
[212] 532-6005

Sheplin Artists & Associates
160 5th Avenue Suite 909
New York, NY 10010
[212] 647-1311

Silver, Massetti & Associates (East) Ltd.
145 West 45th Street #1204
New York, NY 10036
[212] 391-4545

Special Artists Agency, Inc.
111 East 22nd Street Suite 4C,
New York, NY 10010
[212] 420-0200

Peter Strain & Associates, Inc.
1501 Broadway Suite 2900
New York, NY 10036
[212] 391-0380

Talent East
79 5th Avenue
New York, NY 10003
[212] 647-1166

Talent Representatives, Inc.
20 East 53rd Street
New York, NY 10022
[212] 752-1835

The Tantleff Office
375 Greenwich Street Suite 700
New York, NY 10013
[212] 941-3939

Michael Thomas Agency, Inc.
305 Madison Avenue Suite 4419,
NewYork, NY 10165
[212] 867-0303

Tranum, Robertson & Hughes, Inc.
2 Dag Hammarskjold Plaza
New York, NY 10017
[212] 371-7500

Unique Sports Entertainment
& Marketing, Inc.
505 Eighth Avenue Suite 900
New York, NY 10018
[212] 563-6444

Van Der Veer People, Inc.
401 East 57th Street
New York, NY 10022
[212] 688-2880

Waters & Nicolosi
1501 Broadway Suite 1305
New York, NY 10036
[212] 302-8787

Ruth Webb Enterprises, Inc.
445 West 45th Street
New York, NY 10036
[212] 757-6300

Hanns Wolters Theatrical Agency
10 West 37th Street
New York, NY 10018
[212] 714-0100

Ann Wright Representatives, Inc.
165 West 46th Street
New York, NY 10036
[212] 764-6770

Writers & Artists Agency
19 West 44th Street Suite 1000
New York, NY 10036
[212] 391-1112

Zoli Management, Inc.
3 West 18th Street 5th Floor
New York, NY 10011
[212] 242-7490

Ohio Agents

CAM Talent - Cincinatti
1150 West Eighth Street #262
Cincinatti, OH 45203
[513] 421-1795

CAM Talent - Columbus
369 West Third Street
Columbus, OH 45301
[614] 461-0934

168

Creative Talent/Familiar Faces, Inc.
700 Pete Rose Way
Cincinatti, OH 45203
[513] 241-7827
David & Lee, Inc.
757 Statler Office Tower
1127 Euclid Avenue
Cleveland, OH 44115
[216] 522-1300
Goenner Talent
1029 Dublin Road
Columbus, OH 43215
[513] 885-2595
Jo Goenner Talent
P.O. Box 772
10019 Paragon Road
Dayton, OH 45458
[513] 885-2525
Heyman Halper Talent
3308 Brotherton
Cincinatti, OH 45209
[513] 533-3113
Paper Dollz Talent Management, Inc.
1867 West Market Street, Suite C11
Akron, OH 44313
[216] 869-5050
Protocol Model & Talent
1969 North Cleavland-Massillon Road
Akron, Ohio
[216] 666-6066
Colleen Shannon Talent Agency
1384 Grandview Avenue #200
Columbus, OH 43212
[614] 486-0005
Taxi Model Management, Inc.
2044 Euclid Avenue #202
Cleveland, OH 44115
[216] 781-8294

Oregon Agents

Actors Only
2510 SE Belmont
Portland, OR 97214
[503] 233-5073
Cusick's Talent Management
10090 N.W. Hoyt #100
Portland, OR 97209
[503] 274-8555
Rose City Talent
239 NW 13th Avenue, Suite 215
Portland, OR 97209
[503] 274-1005
Wilson Entertainment
037 S.W. Hamilton
Portland, OR 97201
[503] 243-6362

Tennessee Agents

Actors & Others Talent Agency
6676 Memphis - Arlington Road
Bartlett, TN 38134
[901] 385-7885
Buddy Lee Attractions Inc.
38 Music Square E. #300
Nashville, TN 37203
[615] 244-4336
The William Morris Agency, Inc.
2100 West End Avenue, Suite 1000
P.O. Box 37203
Nashville, TN 37215
[615] 385-0310
Talent & Model Land, Inc.
P.O. Box 40763
Nashville, TN 37204
[615] 321-5596

Talent Trek Agency
544 East Broadway
Maryville, TN 37801
[615] 977-8735

Texas Agents

The Campbell Agency
3906 Lemmon Avenue #200
Dallas, TX 75219
[214] 522-8991
Mary Collins Talent Agency
5956 Sherry Lane Suite 917
Dallas, TX 75225
[214] 360-0900
Kim Dawson Agency, Inc.
2710 North Stemmons Freeway #700
Dallas, TX 75207
[214] 630-5161
J&D Talent, Inc.
1825 Market Center Blvd. #320 LB10
Dallas, TX 75207
[214] 744-4411
Marquee Talent, Inc.
2906 Maple Avenue, Suite 21
Dallas, TX 75201
[214] 880-9656
Peggy Taylor Talent, Inc.
1825 Market Center Blvd. #320A
Dallas, TX 75207
[214] 651-7884
Ivett Stone Agency
6309 North O'Connor Road
Suite 116, LB 123
Irving, TX 75039
Actors Etc. Inc.
2620 Fountainview #210
Houston, TX 77057
[713] 785-4495

Intermedia Agency
5353 West Alabama #222
Houston, TX 77056
[713] 622-8282
Pastorini-Bobsy Agency
3013 Fountainview #240
Houston, TX 77057
[713] 266-8282
Quaid Talent Agency
5959 Richmond Avenue #310
Houston, TX 77057
Sherry Young Agency
2620 Fountainview, Suite 212
Houston, TX 77057
[213] 266-5800

Utah Agents

Haile Talent Agency
366 South 500 East Suite 208
Salt Lake City, UT 84102
[801] 532-6961
Rocket Agency
1019 East 2700 South
Salt Lake City, UT 84106
[801] 485-2505

Washington State Agents

Actors & Walker Agency
600 First Avenue #210
Seattle, WA 98104
[206] 682-4368
The Actors Group
114 Alaskan Way South #205
Seattle, WA
[206] 624-9465
Carol James Talent Agency
117 South Main Street
Seattle, WA 98104
[206] 447-9191

Dramatic Artists Agency
1000 Lenora Square #501
Seattle, WA 98104
[206] 442-9190
Lola Hallowell Talent Agency
1700 West Lake Avenue North #436
Seattle, WA 98109
[206] 281-4646
Heffner Management
Westlake Center
1601 Fifth Avenue Suite 2301
Seattle, WA 98101
[206] 622-2211
Eileen Seals Models, International
600 Stewart Street #600 Plaza Building
Seattle, WA 98101
[206] 448-2040
Seattle Models Guild
303 Tower Building
Seattle, WA 98101
[206] 622-1406
Tope Swope Talent Agency
1932 1st Avenue Suite 700
Seattle, WA 98101
[206] 443-2021

Washington, D.C./ Baltimore Agents

Central Casting Inc.
229 North Charles Street
Baltimore, MD 21218
[410] 889-3200

Central Casting Inc.
623 Pennsylvania Avenue S.E.
Washington, DC. 20003
[202] 547-6300
Characters
P.O. Box 73643
Washington, DC 20056
[206] 232-2230

The Erikson Agency
Mclean Professional Park
1483 Chain Bridge Road, Suite 105
Mclean, VA 22101
[703] 356-0040
Kids International
938 East Swan Creek Road, Suite 152
Ft. Washington, MD 20744
[301] 292-7965
Taylor-Royal Casting
2308 South Road
Baltimore, MD 21209
[410] 466-5959

Wisconsin Agents

Jennifer's Talent Unlimited, Inc.
740 N. Plankinton, Suite 300
Milwaukee, Wisconsin 53203-2403
[414] 277-9440
Arlene Wilson Talent, Inc.
809 South 60th Avenue #201
Milwaukee, WI 53214
[414] 778-3838
Lori Lins Ltd.
1301 North Astor Street
Milwaukee, WI 53202
[414] 271-2288
Lori Lins, Ltd.
7611 West Holmes Avenue
Greenfield, WI 53220
[414] 282-3500

CSA CASTING DIRECTORS

Arizona

Darlene Wyatt
1138 East Highland
Phoenix AZ 85014
(602) 263-8650

California

Deborah Aquila
Paramount
5555 Melrose Avenue
Bob Hope Bldg. Suite 200
Los Angeles CA 90038
(213) 956-5444
Maureen Arata
VIACOM
100 Universal City Plaza
Bldg. 506 R104A 104A
Universal City 91608
(818) 777-4410
Deborah Barylski
Disney Studios
500 South Buena Vista
Zorro Bldg. #1 Room 9
Burbamk CA 91521
(818) 560-2896
Fran Bascom
CBS Studio Center
4024 Radford Avenue
Bldg. 5 Room 104
Studio City CA 91604
(818) 760-5895
Pamela Basker
6565 Sunset Blvd. Suite 306
Los Angeles CA 90028
(213) 851-6475

Cheryl Bayer
2020 Avenue of the Stars
5th Floor
Los Angeles CA 90067
Annette Benson
Kushner Locke
11601 Wilshire Blvd. 21st Floor
Los Angeles CA 90025
(310) 445-1111
Chemin Bernard
4435 West Slauson Avenue #146
Los Angeles CA 90043
(213) 507-7400
Juel Bestrop
Gracie Films, Sony Pictures
10202 West Washington Blvd. Poitier Bldg.
Culver City CA 90232
(310) 280-5691
Sharon Bialy
P.O. Box 570308
Tarzana, CA 91358
[818] 342-8630
Tammara Billik
500 South Buena Vista
Trailer 32 Room 2
Burbank, CA 91521
[818] 560-4087
Carissa Blix
Media Casting
6963 Douglas Blvd. #294
Granite Bay CA 95746
[916] 652-3312
Eugene Blythe
Disney Studios
500 South Buena Vista Bldg. 417E
Burbank, CA 91521
[818] 560-7625

172

Megan Brenman
4029 Lankershim Blvd.
Universal City CA 91608
[818] 777-1744

Jacklyn Briskey
NBC Productions
330 Bob Hope Drive
Burbank CA 91523
[818] 840-7727

Mary Buck
4045 Radford Avenue Suite B
Studio City CA 91604
[818] 506 7328

Perry Bullington
3030 Andrita Street Suite A
Los Angeles, CA 90065
[213] 341-5959

Irene Cagen
Lieberman Hirschfield Casting
5979 West 3rd Street Suite 204
Los Angeles CA 90036
[213] 525-1381

Reuben Cannon
1640 South Sepulveda Blvd. Suite 218
Los Angeles CA 90025
[310] 996-1885

Lucy Cavallo
Stephen J. Cannell Productions
7083 Hollywood Blvd.
Hollywood CA 90028
[213] 856-7573

Denise Chamian
Aaron Spelling Productions
5700 Wilshire Blvd. #575
Los Angeles CA 90036

Ellen Chenoeth
Werthemer, Armstrong & Hirsch
1888 Century Park East Suite 1888
Los Angeles CA 90067
[212] 333-4552

Barbara Claman
BCI
8281 Melrose Avenue Suite 300
Los Angeles CA 90046

Lori Cobe
3599 Cahuenga Blvd. West Suite 322
Los Angeles CA 90068
[213] 876-2626

Andrea Cohen
Warner Bros.
4000 Warner Boulevard
Bldg. 5 Room 27
Burbank CA 91522
[818] 954-6709

Annelise Collins
1103 El Centro Avenue
Los Angeles CA 90038
[213] 962-9562

Ruth Conforte
5300 Laurel Canyon Blvd. #168
North Hollywood CA 91607
[818] 760-8220

Allison Cowitt
Mike Fenton & Associates
14724 Ventura Blvd. Suite 510
Sherman Oaks, CA 91403
[818] 501-0177

Billy Damota
P.O. Box 4635
Glendale CA 91222
[818] 243-1263

Anita Dann
270 North Canon Drive Suite 1147
Beverly Hills CA 90210
[310] 278-7765

Eric Dawson
5750 Wilshire Blvd. Suite 250
Los Angeles, CA 90036
[213] 549-0171

Diane Dimeo
12754 Sarah Street
Studio City CA 91604
[818] 505-0945
Pam Dixon
P.O. Box 672
Beverly Hills CA 90213
[310] 271-8064
Donna Dockstader
Universal Studios
100 Universal Plaza
Universal City 91608
[213] 951-9214
Susan Edelman
4045 Radford Avenue Suite B
Studio City CA 91604
[818] 506-7328
Donna Ekholdt
NBC
3000 West Alameda Avenue Suite 231
Burbank CA 91523
[818] 840-4142
Penny Ellers
Aaron Spelling Productions
5700 Wilshire Blvd
North Lobby Suite 116
Los Angeles CA 90036
[213] 525-3524
Mike Fenton
14724 Venture Blvd. Suite 510
Sherman Oaks CA 91403
[818] 501-0177
Steven Fertig
8271 Melrose Avenue #208
Los Angeles CA 90046
[213] 655-5737
Mali Finn
Warner Bros.
4000 Warner Blvd. Trailer 10
Burbank CA 91522
[818] 954-4411

Risa Garcia
Alomar Drive Pictures Inc
517 North Gower Street
Los Angeles CA 90004
[213] 469-7303
David Giella
Reuben Cannon & Associates
1640 South Sepulveda Blvd. Suite 218
Los Angeles CA 90025
[310] 996-1885
Jan Glaser
Concorde-New Horizons
11600 San Vincente Blvd.
Los Angeles CA 90049
[310] 820-6733
Laura Gleason
12400 Ventura Blvd. Suite 312
Studio City CA 91604
[818] 980-5799
Susan Glicksman
5433 Beethoven
Los Angeles CA 90066
[310] 302-9149
Peter Golden
Cannell Productions
7083 Hollywood Boulevard
Hollywood CA 90028
[213] 856-7317
Elisa Goodman
The Mirisch Agency
10100 Santa Monica Blvd Suite 700
Los Angeles CA 90067
[310] 772-0722
Linda Gordon
P.O. Box 461198
Los Angeles, CA 90046
[818] 501-3160

Jeff Greenberg
Paramount
5555 Melrose Avenue
Marx Brothers Bldg. 102
Los Angeles, CA 90038
[213] 956-4886

Harriet Greenspan
9242 Beverly Blvd
Beverly Hills CA 90210
[310] 246-7628

Theodore Hann
Warner Brothers Television
300 Television Plaza
Bldg. 140 Room 139A
Burbank CA 91505
[818] 954-7642

Robert Harbin
2oth Century Fox
10201 West Pico Blvd.
Executive Bldg 335
Los Angeles CA 90035
[310] 203-3847

Karen Hendel
HBO
2049 Century Park East
41st Floor
Los Angeles CA 90067
[310] 201-9309

Cathy Henderson
3025 West Olympic Blvd. Suite 207
Santa Monica CA 90404
[310] 828-7477

Marc Hirschfeld
5979 West 3rd Street Suite 204
Los Angeles CA 90036
[213] 525-1381

Janet Hirshenson
The Casting Company
7461 Beverly Blvd
Los Angeles CA 90036
[213] 938-0700

Alan Hochberg
4063 Radford Avenue #103
Studio City CA 91604
[818] 505-6600

Donna Isaacson
20th Century Fox
10201 West Pico Blvd.
Bldg 12 Room 225
Los Angeles CA 90069

Jane Jenkins
The Casting Company
7461 Beverly Blvd.
Los Angeles CA 90036

Caro Jones
P.O. Box 3329
Los Angeles, CA 90078
[213] 664-0460

Ellie Kanner
Warner Brothers Television
300 South Television Plaza
Building 140
Burbank CA 91505
[818] 954-7644

Darlene Kaplan
P.O. Box 261160
Encino, CA 91426
[818[981-3527

Michael Katcher
5979 3rd Street Suite 204
Los Angeles CA 90036
[213] 525 1381

Marsha Kleinman
704 North Gardner Street #2
Los Angeles CA 90046
[213] 852-1521

Eileen Knight
12009 Guerin Street
Studio City CA 91604
[818] 752-1994

Joanne Koehler
Warner Bros. Television
300 South Television Plaza
Bldg. 140 Room 140
Burbank CA 91505
[818] 954-7636

Shana Landsburg
11811 West Olympic Blvd.
Los Angeles CA 90064
[310] 996-9534

Elizabeth Laroquette
Port Street Films Inc.
4000 Warner Blvd.
Producers Bldg. 1 #102
Burbank CA 91522

John Levey
Warner Bros.
300 South Television Plaza
Bldg 140 Room 138
Burbank CA 91505
[818] 954-4080

Heidi Levitt
1020 North Cole Avenue 2nd Floor
Los Angeles CA 90038
[213] 467-7400

Meg Liberman
5979 West 3rd Street Suite 204
Los Angeles CA 90036
[213] 525-1381

Robin Lippin
NBC
330 Bob Hope Drive Suite C 110
Burbank CA 91523
[818] 840-7643

Molly Lopata
12725 Ventura Blvd. Suite 1
Studio City CA 91604
[818] 753-8086

Junie Johnson Lowry
Paramount
5555 Melrose Avenue
Von Sternberg Suite 104
Los Angeles CA 90038
[213] 956-4856

Bob Macdonald
3030 Andrita Street Suite A
Los Angeles CA 90036
[213] 852-2875

Debi Manwiller
10201 West Pico Blvd
Trailer 767
Los Angeles CA 90035
[310] 203-3153

Mary Margiotta
8265 Sunset Blvd. Suite 200
Los Angeles CA 90046
[213] 650-1760

Irene Mariano
Warner Bros. Television
300 Television Plaza #134A
Burbank CA 91505
[818] 954-7643

Mindy Marin
Casting Artists Inc.
609 Broadway
Santa Monica CA 90401
[310] 395-1882

Valerie Mccaffrey
New Line Cinema
116 North Robertson Blvd. 6th Floor
Beverly Hills CA 90048
[310] 967-6656

Vivian McRae
P.O. Box 1351
Burbank CA 91507
[818] 848-9590

Tom McSweeney
11849 West Olympic Blvd. Suite 101
Los Angeles CA 90064
[310] 273-7773

Barbara Miller
Warner Bros. Television
300 Television Plaza
Bldg. 140 1st Floor
Burbank CA 91505
[818] 954-7645

Bob Morones
KCET
4401 Sunset Blvd.
Los Angeles CA 90027
[213] 953-5657

Helen Mossler
Paramount Television
5555 Melrose Avenue
Los Angeles, CA 90038
[213] 956-5578

Roger Mussenden
20th Century Fox
10201 West Oico Blvd.
Bldg 12 Room 225
Los Angeles CA 90035
[310] 203-1824

Robin Nassif
ABC
2040 Avenue of the Stars
Los Angeles CA 90067
[310] 557-6423

Nancy Nayor
Universal Studios
100 Universal City Plaza
Bldg. 508 1st Floor
Universal City, CA 91608
[818] 777-3566

Gary Oberst
300 North Canon Drive #300
Beverly Hills CA 90210
[310] 273-7773

Lori Openden
NBC
3000 West Alameda Suite 231
Burbank CA 91523
[818] 840-3774

Fern Orenstein
5433 Beethoven
Los Angeles CA 90066
[310] 302-9149

Jeffrey Oshen
Paramount Studios
5555 Melrose Avenue
Gower Mill 117
Los Angeles CA 90038
[213] 956-5969

Jessica Overwise
17250 Sunset Blvd.
Pacific Palisades CA 90272
[310] 459-2686

Richard Pagano
10201 West Pico Blvd.
Trailor 767
Los Angeles CA 90035
[310] 203 3153

Marvin Page
P.O. Box 69964
West Hollywood CA 90069
[818] 760-3040

Linda Phillips Palo
650 North Bronson Avenue Suite 144
Los Angeles CA 90004
[310] 396-8328

John Papsidera
Casting Artists Inc
609 Broadway
Santa Monica CA 90401
[310] 395-1882

Dan Parada
1020 North Cole Avenue Suite 4267
Hollywood CA 90038
[213] 461-3399

Cami Patton
Witt-Thomas Productions
1438 North Gower Street
Bldg 35 Room 577
Los Angeles CA 90028
[213] 960-8276

Donald Pemrick
3520 Hayden Avenue
Culver City CA 90232
[310] 838-7800

Johanna Ray
1022 Palm Avenue Suite 2
West Hollywood CA 90069
[310] 652-2511

Robi Reed
8170 Beverly Blvd Suite 202
Los Angeles CA 90048
[213] 653-6005

Barbara Remsen
650 North Bronson avenue Suite 124
Los Angeles CA 90004
[213] 464-7968

Stu Rosen
7631 Lexington Avenue
Los Angeles CA 90046
[213] 851-1661

Donna Rosenstein
ABC
2040 Avenue of the Stars Suite 500
Los Angeles CA 90067
[310] 557-6423

Marcua Ross
Disney/Touchstone Pictures
500 South Buena Vista
Casting Building
Burbank, CA 91521

David Rubin
8721 Sunset Boulevard Suite 208
Los Angeles CA 90069
[310] 652-4441

Debra Rubenstein
Spelling Entertainment
5757 Wilshire Blvd. Suite 670
Los Angeles CA 90036
[213] 525-2856

Mark Saks
Warner Bros. Television
300 South Television Plaza
Building 140 1st Floor
Burbank CA 91505
[818] 954-7326

Cathy Sandrich
3000 West Olympic Blvd.
Bldg. 2 Room 2572
Santa Monica CA 90404
[310] 264-4138

Ellen Sanitsky
Universal TV
100 Universal City Plaza
Bldg. 463 Room 108
Universal City CA 91608
[818] 777-3023

Susan Scudder
6565 Sunset Blvd. 306
Hollywood CA 90028
[818] 761-7917

Anthony Sepulveda
Warner Bros. Television
300 South Television Plaza
Building 140 Room 137
Burbank CA 91505
[818] 954-7639

Dan Shaner
Wilshire Court Productions, Inc.
1840 Century Park East Suite 400
Los Angeles, CA 90067
[310] 557-2444

178

Barbara Shannon Casting
1536 Rosecrans Suite G
San Diego CA 92106
[619] 224-9555

Melissa Skoff
11684 Ventura Blvd. Suite 5141
Studio City CA 91604
[818] 760-2058

Mary Jo Slater
2500 Broadway
Santa Monica CA 90404
[310] 449-3685

Stanley Soble
Centre Theatre Group
601 West Temple Street
Los Angeles CA 90012
[213] 972-7374

Pamela Sparks
Chelsea
3859 Lankershim Blvd.
Studio City CA 91604
[805] 266-9671

Dawn Steinberg
Big Ticket Television
5700 Wilshire Blvd.
Box 575 Suite 478
Los Angeles CA 90036
[213] 634-5200

Ron Stephenson
MCA Universal Studios
4029 Lankershim Blvd
Building 463 Room 100
Universal City CA 91608
[818] 77-3498

Sally Stiner
12228 Venice Blvd, Suite 503
Los Angeles CA 90066
[310] 827-9796

Randy Stone
20th Century Fox
10201 West Pico Blvd.
Bldg. 54 Room 6
Los Angeles CA 90035
[310] 203-4115

Gilda Stratton
TV Center
6311 Romaine Street # 7219
Los Angeles CA 90038
[213] 962-5575

Monica Swann Casting
12009 Guerin Street
Studio city CA 91604
[818] 769-8564

Judy Taylor
P.O. Box 461198
Los Angeles CA 90046
[818] 501-3160

Mark Teschner
General Hospital
4151 Prospect Avenue
Hollywood CA 90027
[310] 557-5542

Robert Ulrich
6421 Coldwater Canyon
North Hollywood CA 91606
[818] 763-1388

Karen Vice
12001 Ventura Place Suite 203
Studio City CA 91604
[818] 760-5263

Dava Waite
Universal Studios
100 Universal City Plaza
Building 463 Room 104
Universal City CA 91608
[818] 777-1114

Samuel Warren Jr.
2244 4th Avenue Suite D
San Diego CA 92101
[619] 531-0107
Nick Wilkinson
ABC
2040 Avenue of the Stars 5th Floor
Los Angeles CA 90067
[310] 557-6511
Kim Williams
HBO
2049 Century Park East 42nd Floor
Los Angeles CA 90067
[310] 201-9402
Geri Windsor-Fischer
11333 Moorpark Street
P.O. Box 402
Studio City CA 91602
Anne Winthrop
P.O. Box 261160
Encino CA 91426
[818] 981-3527
Dianne Young
15001 Calvert Street
Van Nuys CA 91411
Rhonda Young
10350 Santa Monica Blvd.
Los Angeles CA 90025
[310] 556-2235
Joanne Zaluski
405 South Beverly Drive
Beverly Hills CA 90212
[310] 456-5160
Gary Zuckerbrod
CBS
7800 Beverly Blvd. Suite 284
Los Angeles CA 90036
[213] 852-2835

Florida

Lillian Gordon
13103 Forest Hills Drive
Tampa FL 33162-3335
Yonit Hammer-Tumaroff
Unique Casting Company, Inc.
1613 Alton Road
Miami Beach, FL 33139
Ellen Jacoby
420 Lincoln Road Suite 210
Miami Beach FL 33139
[305] 531-5300
Mel Johnson
1000 Universal City Plaza
Bldg.22 Room 235
Orlando FL 32819
[407] 363-8582
Kathryn Laughlin
Independent Castings Inc.
8313 West Hillsborough Avenue #4
Tampa FL 33615
[813] 884-8335
Cheryl Louden-Kubin
The Casting Crew, Inc.
1948 Tyler Street
Hollywood FL 33020
[305] 927-2329
Beverly McDermott
923 North Golf Drive
Hollywood FL 33021
[305] 625-5111
Dee Miller
742 NE 125th St.
North Miami FL 33161
[305] 895-0339
Lori Wyman
16499 N.E. 19th Avenue Suite 203
North Miami Beach FL 33162
[305] 354-3901

Georgia

Shay Bentley Griffin
Chez Casting, Inc.
572 Armour Circle
Atlanta GA 30324
[404] 873-1215

Illinois

Jane Alderman
2105 North Southport Suite 202
Chicago IL 60614
[312] 549-6464
Jane Brody
20 West Hubbard
Chicago IL 60610
[312] 527-0665

Patricia Collinge
138 Mount Auburn Street
Cambridge MA 02138
[617] 492-4242
Carolyn Pickman
138 Mount Auburn Street
Cambridge MA 02138
[617] 492-4212

Maryland

Pat Moran
805 Park Avenue
Baltimore MD 21201
[410] 385-2107

Minnesota

Jean Rohn
JR Casting
212 3rd Avend North Suite 160
Minneapolis MN 55401-1437
[612] 288-0505

Nevada

Sally Lear
Nevada Casting Group, Inc.
100 Washington
Reno, NV 89503
[702] 322-8187

New York

Alycia Aumuller
Judy Henderson & Associates
330 West 89th Street
New York, NY 10024
[212] 877-0225
Jay Binder
513 West 54th Street
New York NY 10019
[212] 586-6777
Jack Bowdan
Binder Casting
513 West 54th Street
New York NY 10019
[212] 586-6777
Deborah Brown
160 West End Avenue #15P
New York NY 10023
[212] 724-3447
Richard Cole
McCorkle Casting
264 West 40th Street 9th Floor
New York NY 10024
[212] 840-0992
Howard Feur
Altman, Greenfield & Selvaggi
120 West 45th Street 16th Floor
New York NY 10036
Leonard Finger
1501 Broadway Suite 1511
New York NY 10036
[212] 944-8611

Bonnie Finnegan
12 West 27th Street
New York NY 10001
[212] 725-3505

Alexa Fogel Casting
157 Columbus Avenue 2nd Floor
New York NY 10023
[212] 456-3306

Jessica Gilburne
Hugh Moss Casting
311 West 43rd Suite 700
New York NY 10036
[212] 307-6690

Judy Henderson
330 West 89th Street
New York NY 10024
[212] 877-0225

Stuart Howard
22 West 27th Street 10th Floor
New York NY 10001
[212] 725-7770

Phyllis Huffman
Warner Bros.
1325 6th Avenue
New York NY 10036
[212] 636-5023

Julie Hughes
311 West 43rd Street Suite 700
New York NY 10036
[212] 307-6690

Geoffrey Johnson
1501 Broadway Suite 1400
New York NY 10036
[212] 391-2680

Rosalie Joseph
1501 Broadway #2605
New York NY 10036
[212] 921-5781

Lyn Kressel
445 Park Avenue 7th Floor
New York NY 10022
[212]605-9122

Ellen Lewis
130 West 57th Street 12E
New York NY 10019
[212] 245-4635

Vince Liebhart
"As The World Turns"
524 West 57th Street Suite 5330
New York NY 10019
[212] 975-5781

Vincent Liff
1501 Broadway Suite 1400
New York NY 10036
[212] 391-2680

John Lyons
110 West 57th Street 5th Floor
New York NY 10019
[212] 307-1950

Julie Madison
320 West 66th Street
New York NY 10023
[212] 496-3223

Patricia McCorkle
264 West 40th Street
New York NY 10024
[212] 840-0992

Joanna Merlin
The Disney Channel
477 Madison Avenue 5th Floor
New York NY 10022
[212] 735-5342

Elissa Myers
333 West 52nd Street Suite 1008
New York NY 10024
[212] 315-4777

Ellen Novak
20 Jay Street Unit 9B
New York NY 10013
[212] 431-3939

Ellen Parks
Soundstage
630 Ninth Avenue 14th Floor
New York NY 10036

Nancy Piccione
Manhattan Theatre Club
453 West 16th
New York NY 10011
[212] 645-5590

Betty Rea
222 East 44th Street
New York NY 10017
[212] 983-1610

Liz Woodman
11 Riverside Drive #2 JE
New York NY 10023
[212] 787-3782

Andrew Zerman
Johnson Liff Casting
1501 Broadway Suite 1400
New York NY 10036
[212] 391-2680

Pennsylvania

Donna Belajac
247 Fort pitt Boulevard
Pittsburgh PA 15222
[412] 391-1005

Tennessee

Jo Doster
P.O. Box 120641
Nashville TN 37212-0641
[615] 385-3850

Texas

Jo Edna Boldin
Third Coast Casting
Studio B Productions
501 North IH 35
Austin TX 78702
[512] 472-4247

Barbara Brinkley
P.O. Box 167157
Irving TX 75016
[214] 986-0427

Liz Keigley
121 North Hall
Sugarland TX
[713] 242-7265

Rody Kent
5422 Vickery Blvd.
Dallas TX 75206
[214] 827-3418

Utah

Cate Praggastis
Take One Casting
5480 South Woodcrest Drive
Salt Lake City UT 84117
[801] 461-5843

Washington

Jodi Rothfield
2033 6th Avenue Suite 306
Seattle WA 98121
[206] 448-0927

Patti Kalles Casting
506 Second Avenue
Smith Tower 1525
Seattle WA 98104

Breakdown Services, Ltd.
P.O. Box 69277
Los Angeles, CA 90069
[213] 276-9166

Pacific Coast Directory
6313 Yucca Street
Hollywood, CA 90028-5093
[213] 469-3564

Drama-Logue
P.O.Box 38771
Los Angeles, CA 90038-0771
Tel [213] 464-5079

Daily Variety
5700 Wilshire Blvd Ste 120
Los Angeles, CA 90036
TEL [800] 552-3632

Backstage
1515 Broadway, 14th Floor
New York, NY 10036
(212) 536-5176

Samuel French Bookstore
76223 Sunset Blvd.
Hollywood, CA 90046
[213] 876-0570

Acting World Books
P.O. Box 3044
Hollywood, CA 90078
(The Agencies, etc.)

Photoscan
646 Bryn Mawr St.
Orlando, Florida
32804

Actors Equity Association
165 West 46th St.
15th Floor
New York, NY 10019-5214
(212) 869-8530

AFTRA
6922 Hollywood Blvd.
HOLLYWOOD, CA 90078
[213] 461-8111

Screen Actors Guild
5757 Wil;shire Blvd.
Los Angeles, 90036
(213) 954-1600
Conservatory [213] 856-7736

Recommended Reading

Acker, Iris. *The Secrets of Auditioning for Commercials.*

Adler, Stella. *The Technique of Acting.*

Charles, Jill. *Directory of Professional Theatre Training Programs, Regional Theatre Directory, Summer Theatre Directory.*

Cohen, Robert. *Acting Professionally.*

Eaker, Sherry. *The Backstage Handbook for Performing Artists.*

Friedman, Ginger. *The Perfect Monologue.*

Goldman, William. *Adventures in the Screen Trade.*

Henry, Mari Lyn & Rogers, Lynne. *How to be a Working Actor.*

Hornby, Richard. *The End of Acting.*

Jaroslaw, Mark. *The Actor's Handbook: Seattle & The Pacific Northwest.*

Lewis, M.K. and Rosemary. *Your Film Acting Career.*

Linklater, Kristin. *Freeing the Natural Voice.*

Litvak, Mark. *Reel Power.*

McGaw, Charles. *Acting is Believing.*

Monos, Jim. *Professional Actor Training in New York City.*

Stanislavski, Konstantin. *An Actor Prepares, My Life in Art, Building a Character.*

Shurtleff, Michael. *Audition!*

Wolper, Andrea. *The Actor's City Sourcebook.*

Seminars by Andrew Reilly

For information on seminars and workshops
given by the author, write to:

RAM Communications
P.O. Box 545918
Surfside, FL 33154
[305] 868-9709

How to Order additional copies of *An Actor's Business*

Have autographed copy of this book sent to
yourself or to the person of your choice.
Send $18.95 plus
$2.00 shipping to:

RAM COMMUNICATIONS
P.O. Box 545918
Surfside, FL 33154

Or call
(800) 360-4511
and use your credit card.